Death in
Glacier National Park
Stories of Accidents and Foolhardiness in the
Crown of the Continent

Randi Minetor

Guilford, Connecticut

An imprint of Rowman & Littlefield

Distributed by NATIONAL BOOK NETWORK

Copyright © 2016 by Rowman & Littlefield

All rights reserved. No part of this book may be reproduced in any form or by any electronic or mechanical means, including information storage and retrieval systems, without written permission from the publisher, except by a reviewer who may quote passages in a review.

British Library Cataloging in Publication Information Available

Library of Congress Cataloging-in-Publication Data
Names: Minetor, Randi, author.
Title: Death in Glacier National Park : stories of accidents and foolhardiness in the crown of the continent / Randi Minetor.
Description: Guilford, Connecticut : Lyons Press, [2016] | Includes bibliographical references and index.
Identifiers: LCCN 2016001012 | ISBN 9781493024001 (pbk. : alk. paper) | ISBN 9781493025473 (electronic)
Subjects: LCSH: Accidents—Glacier National Park (Mont.)—Anecdotes. | Violent deaths—Glacier National Park (Mont.)—Anecdotes. | Bear attacks—Glacier National Park (Mont.)—Anecdotes. | Glacier National Park (Mont.)—History—Anecdotes.
Classification: LCC F737.G5 M55 2016 | DDC 978.6/52—dc23 LC record available at http://lccn.loc.gov/2016001012

CONTENTS

PREFACE

THIS BOOK DETAILS MANY OF THE 264 DEATHS THAT HAVE taken place in Glacier National Park since the staff began keeping records in 1913, three years after Glacier became a unit of the National Park Service. I have endeavored to research every incident, but some—particularly those involving heart attacks or "natural causes"—were not covered by the media or chronicled in park documents. Other events (including a number of drowning accidents) must have been cataclysmic to the families involved, but they did not generate the media interest at the time to help me tell a detailed story today. In these cases you will find listed in this book's appendix the names, dates, and areas of the park in which the death occurred, but no other details in the chapters. If I appear to have skipped over your ancestor or loved one, I most likely could not find much information about his or her demise. Please feel free to get in touch with me at author@ minetor.com to provide any factual information you may have, so I can include it in the next edition.

As you read this book, please keep in mind that an average of only 2.6 people per year lose their lives during a visit to Glacier—and with 2,238,761 people visiting the park in 2014, this makes your odds of dying in the park about 861,062 to 1. Please do not take this concentration of stories as an indication that this spectacular park is a place to be feared. Instead, see them as the cautionary tales they are, further reinforcement of the basic rules of safety the National Park Service asks you to follow during your visit. (You'll find these rules and other survival tips in the Epilogue.)

Let me take this opportunity to encourage you, to urge you, even to insist that you plan a trip to northwestern Montana to enjoy Glacier National Park. Few places on the planet parallel its vast wilderness, the startling majesty of its high peaks, and its opportunities for views of "charismatic mega-fauna," the large animals that people come from all over the world to see. This glacially carved landscape reminds us of the forces well beyond our own that first sculpted such magnificent places, and the responsibility we all have to preserve pristine environments like this one. I can't tell you how pleased you will be that you took the risk—the truly infinitesimal risk—and made the trip to one of America's wildest places.

INTRODUCTION:
A GREAT VACATION GONE WRONG

THE STORIES YOU ARE ABOUT TO READ ARE ALL TRUE. SOME involve a little speculation about what may have transpired to cause the death in each case, but I have endeavored to be as factual as the media coverage and history allow.

There is no kinder way to describe what's in this book: These are stories about people going to a magnificent place expecting to have the time of their lives, and coming home dead. That being said, this book also brings to light the impressive facts of the massive search and rescue operations involved in attempting to save the lives of people who find themselves in trouble in Glacier National Park.

These are stories of daring rescues, uncommon teamwork, remarkable skill, and the many heroes throughout northwestern Montana who dedicate their professional and volunteer time to saving lives, or to recovering the bodies of people who have perished, so their loved ones can bring closure to their ordeal of loss. My research focused on those who died, but the park's records also are filled with stories of successful rescues—testaments to the training and courage of the rangers of the National Park Service, Flathead County Search and Rescue, North Valley Search and Rescue, Flathead Nordic Ski Patrol, Mountain Rescue Team, Two Bear Air, ALERT Air Ambulance at the Kalispell Regional Medical Center, the US Border Patrol, the US Forest Service, and the Flathead County Sheriff's Office. Together, this suite of rescue services handles more than five hundred calls every year, all but a handful of whose lives are saved. They are part of the reason that Glacier actually has one of the lower death rates in the National Park Service system, given the park's size—nearly one million acres—and the number of visitors it draws (well over two million) on an annual basis.

Death in Glacier National Park is also the story of journalists, especially the ones who braved the risks of the wilderness to bring readers the most extensive coverage of these events. My hat is off to the writers at the *Daily Inter Lake,* the *Independent Record,* the *Missoulian,* and others whose excellent work gives us insights into the famous Night of the Grizzlies in 1967; the avalanches of 1953 and 1969; the disappearances and eventual discovery of pilot Donald Donovan and his passenger, Kathy See, and hikers Jake Rigby, Jakson Kreiser, and Yi-Jien Hwa; and the searches for Joseph and William Whitehead, F. H. Lumley, James Pinney, John Provine, and others whose remains may still linger somewhere in the park.

You will find all of these incidents treated with respect, even though some of them warrant a private guffaw at the misguidedness of people who venture off into the treacherous Glacier backcountry without carrying so much as a packet of trail mix, who ignore warning signs and guardrails as if the laws of physics do not apply to them, or who believe that climbing one of the park's highest mountains in the dead of winter ranks as an entry-level adventure.

Most of the people who have died in Glacier encountered sheer bad luck—a stepping stone that looked stable and turned out to be slick, an icy crevasse hidden by new-fallen snow, or a boulder careening down from a rock face of its own volition. Others took precautions they considered adequate, without a true understanding of the danger present. It's one thing to stop and take photos of bears, for example, and quite another to fail to recognize that the advancing bear seen through your viewfinder is a wild animal about to attack. These people are not so much foolish as naïve, lacking an understanding of nature as *natural*, and therefore distinctly different from the tightly controlled environment of an Orlando theme park.

You will see the words "cautionary tale" in several places in this book, as I see these factual accounts as crystallized reminders that nature is a stronger force than humanity. Read these stories and take the lessons they provide to heart, with the understanding that in each case there is a misstep, a moment at which the result could go the safe way or another way. Mindfulness of the potential for these miscalculations will help you avoid such consequences in your own visit to Glacier, making your trip to this spectacular wilderness as exciting as you wish—but with just a little less danger, a little more self-awareness, and a great deal more fun.

If, in the end, this book encourages you to see more of Glacier National Park just to get a glimpse of the roaring waterfalls, precarious ledges, high peaks, and sheer drop-offs that led to the deaths of people in this book, then *Death in Glacier National Park* has done its job. I urge you to explore this park to the extent that your personal abilities will allow, whether you experience it primarily by car or tour bus or you take to the trails and see the backcountry in all of its natural glory. Venture beyond Going-to-the-Sun Road to see Two Medicine and Many Glacier, and head north to Polebridge, Goat Haunt, and Waterton Lakes National Park in Canada. Peer over the cliff along the Garden Wall or marvel at the rushing water of McDonald Creek or the North Fork of the Flathead River, but take every precaution to be sure that you come home with the ability to tell the tale.

Don't give me the dubious opportunity to write about your untimely demise in the next edition of this book. Enjoy Glacier with your gear on your belt or in your backpack, heed the advice given by rangers who know this park better than you do, and watch your step when the scree gets brittle. Go, dear readers, to the Crown of the Continent. See this magnificent place—and do it safely.

CHAPTER 1

Treacherous Waters:
A Long History of Drowning

Gregory Warren Allenby Trenor probably shared the characteristics of most six-year-old boys who visit Glacier National Park with their parents. We can guess that during his visit on June 27, 1963, the beauty of the scenery and foliage surrounding him were largely lost on the child, but that the search for small frogs and salamanders along McDonald Creek, the possible glimpse of a trout, and the antics of diving harlequin ducks and American dippers all fascinated him no end. When he, his father, Cameron, and his brothers, Douglas and Melvin, left their car at a turn-off on Going-to-the-Sun Road at around six p.m. to get a close look at McDonald Falls, we can guess that Gregory hopped from rock to rock along the creek bank under the watchful eye of his father. "The party walked upstream to the trail bridge which crosses McDonald Creek," the story in Kalispell's newspaper, the *Daily Inter Lake*, read the next day. "Then they walked beneath the bridge and along the bank."

In most areas of the country, a waterway the length, width, and depth of McDonald Creek would qualify as a river. Varying in width depending on the season, this so-called creek roars with frothy meltwater well into July, cascading mightily down drops of fifteen feet or more at Upper and Lower McDonald Falls. Many visitors pause along the creek to marvel at its ferocity—and when they are seized by the sense of daring that often grips tourists when they explore a national park as grand as Glacier, many pick their way along the rocks to points much too close for safety.

So when the stable surface below his feet suddenly became slippery, Gregory didn't know how to recover or what to grab. Perhaps he shrieked for help, or maybe the fall took him so by surprise that he slid into the water without a sound. He could not have known that the swiftly flowing creek had swelled with snowmelt more recently than any creek at home—in fact, snow still clung to many peaks throughout Glacier National Park in these waning days of June. The only thing Gregory knew was that the water was icy cold, numbing his extremities in no time and carrying him away on the ceaseless current.

What went through Cameron's mind as he saw his son disappear into the churning waters? Instinct undoubtedly overrode the hard logic that would have told him that the boy's fate was already sealed. Like any father would, Cameron plunged headlong into the water with nothing on his mind but a desperate attempt to save the boy. Just as Gregory went numb seconds after the creek claimed him, however, Cameron also realized with a start that this frigid mountain water—thirty-eight degrees Fahrenheit that day, according to the *Montana Standard* newspaper—would stiffen his joints and freeze his limbs. Worse, his son was nowhere in sight. He had no choice but to get back to shore and find help as fast as he possibly could.

Water temperature in Glacier's two hundred–plus lakes and more than fifteen hundred miles of streams, creeks, and rivers never gets above fifty degrees at the surface, and the water remains colder as it gets deeper. Some of the lakes, including Lake McDonald—at the mouth of McDonald Creek—are several hundred feet deep at their lowest points. As Gregory drifted along with the current toward Lake McDonald, he was headed for the deepest, coldest lake in the park.

When Cameron and his family reached a ranger and told him what had happened, park staff members went to work immediately. "Our crews got out on the search right away," park public information officer Dan Nelson told the newspaper. "One of the rangers, Robert Sellers, was teaching a first aid class at headquarters. The 30 people in the class were divided into two groups and began searching for the body immediately. We also called immediately for members of the Flathead County Search and Rescue unit—the SCUBA divers."

The Flathead County Lifesaving and Rescue Association, still in operation today, is trained in virtually any form of rescue required in the park. Formed in 1947, the association began as a group of World War II veterans looking to serve a critical need for skilled rescue personnel in the rugged, mountainous terrain in and around the Flathead Valley and Glacier National Park. On the day Gregory Trenor fell into McDonald Creek, twelve of the rescue squad's scuba divers began to explore the waterways—seven in McDonald Creek and five at the creek's mouth in Lake McDonald—in the hope of giving the grieving family the comfort of laying their loved one to rest.

Among these experienced divers were Tom Dumay, a twenty-one-year-old lifesaving diver from nearby Columbia Falls and a senior at Montana State University, and Ron Koppang, a diver of the same age who also lived in Columbia Falls. Working together, they began their search for Gregory by exploring a series of ledges in McDonald Creek, in hopes of recovering the boy's body in shallower waters. The crews worked into the night, calling off the search at ten thirty p.m. when it became too dark, and beginning again at four a.m. on Friday, June 28. Dumay and Koppang then began searching in a deeper part of the lake.

Neither of the young men was prepared for the sudden force of a waterfall below the lake's surface—a phenomenon created by a blast of current from the creek surging as it tumbled over McDonald Falls.

"Koppang said he and Dumay were about 60 feet below the surface when their aqualung tanks began running short of air," the *Montana Standard* and the *Butte Daily Post* reported the following day. "He said they had started to surface when they were caught in a terrific current which officials described as an 'underwater cascade' below the delta where the creek flows into the lake."

Fighting for his life, Koppang managed to grab Dumay and start for the surface, but the current broke his grasp, pushing both divers well below the sixty-foot level—down as far as one hundred forty feet. Koppang had no choice but to rush to the surface to save his own life, emerging near the mouth of the creek. The other members of the rescue team waited to see Dumay's yellow oxygen tanks coming up from far below. Seconds passed, and then minutes, but Dumay did not rise.

The team could come to only one conclusion: Tom Dumay had drowned.

Koppang emerged in rough shape. His sudden return to the surface had triggered a case of the "bends," the extremely painful, often fatal sickness caused by the pressure of nitrogen bubbles in his system that his body had not had time to expel. Accompanied by his father, he was rushed in a pressurized aircraft to a decompression chamber at Brownlee Dam in Idaho, where he would spend the next thirty-eight hours under close supervision as his body pressure returned to normal.

With the rescue and recovery team fractured and no sign of the six-year-old boy, Chief Ranger Lyle McDowell came to the inevitable conclusion that Gregory's body was too far down in the lake for the divers to find safely. He called off the search for the child and turned the team's attention to finding the body of Tom Dumay. Now the divers used heavier tanks and lines to keep another tragedy from happening as they searched for their colleague. Two of the divers, Don Elgin and Jack Von Lindern, discovered Dumay about one hundred feet below the lake's surface and brought him up with them late in the afternoon.

While the underwater search for Gregory Trenor ended that day, no one had any intention of giving up on finding the

"Officials report that visual observations will be made during the next few days in anticipation that the youth's body will surface during that period," the *Daily Inter Lake* reported on Sunday, June 30. "Officials indicate that it is possible, but not probable, that the body might still be in McDonald Creek."

For the next several weeks, rangers made morning and afternoon checks of the area near the mouth of the creek, using a grappling hook to attempt to find the child's remains. These twice-daily checks revealed nothing, however, and eventually the rangers lengthened the time between their attempts, checking every few days instead of daily. Park staff began to assume that this body, like others from previous drowning accidents, might not emerge at all.

Then on Wednesday, August 21, park resident Eugene Fox contacted Glacier park headquarters to report something unusual: a white tennis shoe wedged behind a boulder, about four feet below the surface of Lake McDonald and about a mile from the spot where Gregory had fallen into the creek.

Park staff moved quickly to investigate. Sure enough, the sneaker was still on Gregory's foot, and the park had the opportunity to send the child's body home to his family in Seattle and bring them some closure at the end of this tragedy.

THE NUMBER-ONE CAUSE OF DEATH

Glacier National Park contains 762 lakes and 563 streams, according to a 2013 article in the *Great Falls Tribune*. This alone provides one reason that fifty-eight people have drowned to date within park boundaries since Glacier became a national park in 1910—in fact, more people have died in these lakes, rivers, and creeks than in any other manner in the park.

The remarkable number of water features only partially explains so many deaths, however. As Cameron Trenor discovered and as many other would-be rescuers quickly determine once they leap into the water to save a loved one, Glacier's waters are some of the coldest on the continent. Surface temperatures can remain just above freezing for most of the year, and even July and August sunshine can't heat the lakes' surfaces above fifty degrees Fahrenheit. The creeks and streams that feed into the lakes are fueled by snowmelt from the park's many high peaks—so even in the hottest part of the summer, these waterways maintain frigid temperatures.

Cold is just one of the threats that can overpower visitors who slip and fall into a rushing stream. Many of Glacier's creeks swell with snowmelt and storm runoff from the mountains throughout the spring and summer, so even a fairly quiet stream can surge unexpectedly when a sheet of snow gives way from miles off. An abrupt wave in a roiling creek can knock a person off his feet, if the fast-moving water alone has not already done so. Such surges can occur in lakes as well; the underwater waterfall that surprised Tom Dumay and Ron Koppang in 1963 is just one case in point that demonstrates the dangerous nature of Glacier's waters.

The intelligent tourist who respects these streams and lakes will have no life-threatening mishaps, however. The stories in this chapter all emphasize the same precautions for your and your family's safety: Keep a close eye on children to be sure they don't approach rushing streams, watch your own footing as you visit waterfalls and creeks, and wear a life jacket if you decide to take a boat out to the middle of a lake.

In this chapter you'll find tales of death by water that I have brought together according to the many different ways one can drown in Glacier National Park: fording streams, sinking a boat, attempting to rescue others, fishing from rocky ledges, and a few that are just sheer bad luck. With so many stories to tell, this selection provides a way to grasp the lessons we can learn from so many who have perished in the park—and what situations require special precautions when you plan your own visit to this magnificent place.

HORSE SENSE

The first person to drown in Glacier National Park fell from her horse while attempting to ford what the *Allentown Leader*, the newspaper of her hometown in Pennsylvania, called "a small stream." Jane Davis was visiting Glacier at the end of June 1916 when she took the horseback ride that would prove fatal. We don't know all the details, but the stream that took her life emptied into the Two Medicine River, where Davis's body was recovered a day later.

Davis was not the only equestrian ever to perish in the park because of an ill-conceived ford. In 1954, eighteen-year-old Pat Kays headed out to Lake Sherburne on horseback with the goal of riding out to Cracker Flat to retrieve horses grazing near the lake. An experienced horse wrangler who worked for the Wellman riding horse concession near Many Glacier Hotel that summer, Kays clearly felt confident enough to attempt a deepwater fording of Canyon Creek, a waterway that empties into Lake Sherburne.

When he did not return by that evening, the other wranglers and park staff began a search for Kays that eventually included thirty men, two boats, airplanes, and a bloodhound, according to the *Daily Inter Lake*. The rescue force found Kays's horse near the creek with its reins tangled around its neck, and soon discovered the boy's cowboy hat on the bank, along with horse tracks that indicated that the horse had entered the water slowly and come out of it in a hurry— a sign that the horse had been somehow frightened in the water. Five days later grappling hooks brought up Kays's body in Lake Sherburne, about one hundred yards from the spot where he had attempted to cross the creek on horseback— a point where the water would have been deep enough to cover the boy's head, even as he sat astride his horse. Park staff speculated that the depth and temperature of the icy water might have spooked the horse into throwing Kays off its back.

A Curious Chronicle of Lives Lost

In 1923, eighteen-year-old Samantha Jones traveled to Glacier on a geology expedition, apparently related to her studies at the University of Wisconsin. No details are available to explain how she came to be flailing for her life in Lake McDonald, but she and a young man of about the same age, Fred W. Huber, both drowned on the same day. To this day their bodies remain somewhere in the ten-mile-long lake.

On July 4, 1924, park concessions worker Donald T. Fly lost his life in St. Mary Lake, one of many seasonal park employees who may have ignored all the suggested precautions when he ventured out into the lake. As we will see in many instances throughout this book, seasonal concessions employees often find themselves taking on more challenge than they would normally consider were they not working in a rugged national park alongside people with far more experience in the wilderness.

Such was the case in June 1977 when twenty-two-year-old Randy Hill, a seasonal employee from Mount Morris, Michigan, and twenty-year-old David Noel Barry, who came from Falls Church, Virginia, went swimming on a Thursday night in Wilbur Creek at the foot of a waterfall. "Two sisters who were with the victims, Tarisa and Mary Ann Guderian of Covinton, La., told park rangers the four had been sliding over the waterfall into the creek when the two men were drawn back under the falls about 10 p.m. Thursday," the *Daily Inter Lake* reported on June 26, 1977.

Swept behind the falls and held underwater by the force of the cascade, the two young men could not fight their way to the surface. Divers found Randy's body on Friday afternoon in the deep pool, and David's about seventy feet away, still in the creek.

James Larson, an eighteen-year-old from Forest City, Iowa, spent his second summer in 1954 in charge of motor- and rowboats at the Many Glacier Hotel. Perhaps he wanted the job so much that he hid from his employers that he could not swim, or maybe he truly believed that if push ever came to shove he would survive by instinct. When he slipped while closing a window on a boat and fell into the lake, however, he realized instantly the severity of his error. He yelled for help and got it—people came running to his aid and pulled him out of the water within five minutes—but during his ordeal in the water, he hit his head on the bottom of the boat. The blow knocked him out, and even though a doctor staying at the hotel worked for nearly three hours to revive him, she could not bring him around.

COMPOUND TRAGEDIES

Perhaps Lena Longini, a nineteen-year-old woman hiking with her younger brother, Henry, and some friends along the St. Mary River in July 1925, should have selected more resourceful companions. When the group stopped to admire St. Mary Falls, twelve-year-old Henry climbed up some rocks to reach the perfect vantage point for a photograph. He stopped to snap the picture, lost his balance, and fell into the plunge pool at the bottom of the falls. "An instant later the boy was struggling bravely for his life," the story in the *Portsmouth Daily Times* of Ohio tells us. "Never hesitating, his sister poised for a moment on the brink of the pool and then dived. But her courage was unavailing. Desperately she fought through the water to her brother. As she battled she shouted words of encouragement, which could plainly be heard by the onlookers. Before she reached him, the boy disappeared from sight."

Overcome with cold and with the pounding of the falls, Lena sank as well. Their friends, standing by without offering any assistance, finally decided to contact a ranger when both Lena and Henry vanished into the pool. By then, however, their fate had been sealed. Both the girl and her brother died on the spot.

Not all such rescues were complete failures, though some came with their share of tragedy. When eight-year-old Mary Barbara Lee fell into McDonald Creek in the summer of 1949, her father, Major Fred P. Lee of the US Army, leaped into the water to save her. He succeeded in locating her in the pounding rapids and bringing her to the creek bank, but he himself succumbed to the current and was swept away. At the time of his death, the forty-eight-year-old veteran was stationed with the quartermaster corps in Chicago, according to the *Salt Lake Tribune*.

Elberta Dickman fared no better in her attempt to save her fifteen-year-old daughter, Mary Jo. When the family—including Elberta's husband, Francis, and her older daughter, Kathleen—stopped at a pull-off on Going-to-the-Sun Road on a late June afternoon in 1962 and walked down the incline to McDonald Creek, Mary Jo slipped and fell into the water. Her mother tried to reach out to her from shore, but she also lost her balance and fell forward into the water, striking her head on a rock. The current swept Elberta away, and we can assume that her husband rescued Mary Jo in the interim as a passerby contacted Ranger Fred Wood at Lake McDonald Ranger Station. Ranger Wood came to the scene and found Mrs. Dickman in the water about two hundred yards from where she had fallen. He did his best to try to resuscitate her until a doctor could arrive, but Elberta never regained consciousness.

On August 3, 1952, Frank B. Stewart, a retired Edison Company employee visiting Glacier from Alhambra, California, stood fishing on a large, flat rock at the base of St. Mary Falls when he slipped and fell twenty feet into the plunge pool. At first it seemed he might be rescued, as Dr. D. B. Parker of Ness City, Kansas, saw Stewart fall and rushed to the site to help him. Dr. Parker did not attempt to swim—the papers report that this was not among his skills—but he threw the flailing Stewart his fishing line and began to pull him in toward shore. The line could not hold the weight of an adult man, however, especially one fighting the strong current the waterfall churned up just a few feet away. In a moment the line snapped, and Stewart did his best to hold his own for a few moments before the swirling water swept him under. "The first time out from under a ledge he was still swimming, but the second time he floated out face down and downstream, according to Dr. Parker," reported the *Daily Inter Lake*. Parker ran to notify park authorities, and a crew set out to recover Stewart's body, soon finding him pinned against a tree by the water's power.

When their nine-year-old nephew fell into Upper McDonald Creek on July 27, 1981, both Donald and Betty Danielowski leaped in after him to do their best to save him. Their efforts were successful in one sense—the boy survived—but his aunt and uncle, aged forty-one and thirty-six, both succumbed to the current and the cold. The couple from the town of Mound, Minnesota, were the second and third person to drown in Glacier that week: Just a few days before, on July 22, seven-year-old Kevin Dolack, visiting from Glenview, Illinois, with his family, slipped off a rock near the footbridge and fell into the same creek. The creek's force swept him away in an instant.

Over the decades, slipping and falling into Glacier's waters became the refrain most often heard by rescue crews and rangers. Many local visitors or vacationers slid into creeks or lakes when their footwear gave way on water-slick rocks. While full details are not available for every case, we can extrapolate from the facts we do know: Many of these unlucky tourists obeyed the park's rules and stayed on footpaths and bridges or behind defined lines, but in a moment of distraction as they took photos or leaned out for a better view, they lost their footing.

For Want of a Flotation Device

The use of life jackets for fishing and other water sports would not come into common practice until after World War II, so perhaps it's not surprising that a number of the early drowning deaths in Glacier took place when boats capsized or sank.

Stanley Clark, a thirty-three-year-old national park employee from Sebeka, Minnesota, drowned in St. Mary Lake in June 1931 when his boat overturned during an evening ride. The boat dumped Clark and four companions into the water, and the other four swam for shore and reached it safely. Clark, however, could not make it to shore before the cold water overcame him.

An even greater tragedy on a Glacier lake occurred in 1934, when a boat carrying seven members of the Civilian Conservation Corps—the workforce created by President Franklin Roosevelt to give people meaningful employment during the Great Depression—launched from the dock at Lake Sherburne to carry lunch to crews working in the Many Glacier wilderness. Hardly had the boat pulled away from the dock when it inexplicably listed to one side and began to sink. News reports note that the boat could hold twenty passengers, so the seven aboard should have been a light load—and with the boat still close to the dock, we can only assume that not all of the passengers could swim. Four of them escaped the lake's icy water, but three did not: an M. Greppo Jr. from Schenectady, New York; A. Montemarano of Brooklyn, New York; and Gilbert Cooper, who came from Ronan, Montana. No ages were listed for these men, although most of the CCC workers in the park were in their late teens and early twenties. Park staff retrieved the boat three days later.

Up on Kintla Lake, just below the Canadian border on the west side of the park, three men on a fishing vacation went missing on September 13, 1950, when one of two things may have happened: Either their aluminum boat capsized during a sudden storm or the outboard motor fell off the boat and the men tried to retrieve it in the super-chilled water. Camping on the side of the lake, the three men— Aubrey Clyde Olinger, James Pinney, and John Provine, all in their late thirties—began their fishing trip on Tuesday of that week, following the pattern most fishermen use on Kintla Lake, "fishing up to the head along the south shore and then returning to camp by a bee-line down the middle of the six-mile lake," the *Daily Inter Lake* explained. The Wednesday storm may have taken them by surprise, sending waves crashing over the side of their small craft, a situation that would have prevented them from rowing or motoring back to their camp. Alternatively, if their motor fell off the boat of its own accord, it would have sunk to the bottom—a distance not charted or calculated for some parts of Kintla Lake—making it impossible for the fishermen to retrieve it.

They may have tried anyway, however, soaking themselves with water just above the freezing point and allowing themselves to develop hypothermia, a condition that could kill them within hours.

Olinger's body came to light when a couple from nearby Stryker, who were fishing in the area, came across the half-submerged boat with Olinger still in it, fully dressed except for his shoes and with one foot caught under a seat. The boat's outboard motor was gone, and most of their fishing gear showed up on the north shore, across the lake and several miles from their campsite.

Provine's and Pinney's bodies never came to the surface. In a cold lake like Kintla, park superintendent Jack Emmert told the *Daily Inter Lake*, "bodies submerged in Glacier Park lakes usually do not come to the top for three or four weeks because of the extremely cold water," which does not rise above the warmer water at the surface. Search crews continued to survey the area until snow arrived in October, but to this day, the remains of the two men remain hidden somewhere along the bottom of the lake.

Rafting—whether as a feat of daring over Glacier's class V rapids, or more gently as a float trip in calmer waters—has become very popular in the park, but in the 1970s many rafters believed that life jackets were too cumbersome to wear or that flotation devices were for sissies. This attitude began to change as the park racked up casualties among those who did not fully understand the power of Glacier's mighty creeks and rivers.

On June 29, 1970, five Columbia Falls men in their early twenties set off to raft the North Fork of the Flathead River in a rubber vessel, probably expecting a fairly easy ride even though the river had swelled with high country rainwater. When the raft snagged on a logjam a mile and a half south of Polebridge, branches sticking out of the logs tore into the raft and deflated it, dumping its passengers into the river. Four of them swam for safety and managed to reach an island in the middle of the river, but twenty-three-year-old Robert Personett, a US Navy man home on leave, became wrapped up in the deflating raft and could not swim for shore. He sank with the raft, becoming further tangled in another logjam that held his body underwater.

Personett's companions, Robert Kluka, Gene Halles, Arthur Ott, and Michael Ren, remained on the island for nearly twenty-four hours while they waited for a passing boater or ranger to spot them and report their whereabouts. Once they were safely on the mainland, a rescue crew from the Flathead County Lifesaving and Rescue Association began to work with park personnel to locate Personett's body.

Two days of intensive searching by divers and park staff members in boats did not produce Personett. Calling off the mission for two days in hopes that water levels would go down, the recovery team resumed on Sunday, July 5, with four divers and jet boats to support them. "Visibility in the high, muddy river was only three or four feet at most," the *Montana Standard* reported on Tuesday, July 7. "Officials say the search will be resumed in about a week."

Nine days later, as the park used boats, aircraft, and periodic checks of the shoreline by searchers on foot, Personett's body still had not risen to the surface. Fluctuating water levels and obstacles in the water managed to capsize and stove in one of the recovery boats, plunging rescue personnel Keight Wulfgram, Eric Krueger, and Jack Polzin into the water and sending one of the park's shortwave radios to the bottom of the Flathead River. All three made it safely to shore, though Wulfgram sustained some minor injuries as he tangled with some of the branches in the offending logjam.

"It's a rough task," said mission coordinator Ed Trippet to the *Daily Inter Lake* on July 23. "The river is still running high, but water levels have fallen. There are numerous logjams. Every time it rains in the high country you can count on murky water, but we'll make the attempt again anyhow."

As recovery attempts continued into the end of July, "Ed Trippet, coordinator of the mission, reported it was not entirely fruitless," the *Daily Inter Lake* noted on July 27. "Divers found a 26-foot canoe with equipment wrapped around a rock near Blankenship's Bridge. This was retrieved and brought to the Flathead County Sheriff's Office where the owner can claim it." At earlier points in the search, divers disassembled a logjam and found a tent and a sleeping bag.

Finally, on Saturday, August 8, at about four p.m., a family search headed by Richard P. Walsh, superintendent of the Montana Soldiers Home, discovered Personett's body about two miles north of Coal Creek, roughly ten miles from the point at which the raft sank on June 29. Its location was so remote that a recovery crew had to be dispatched to bring the body downriver two miles to a point at which it could be evacuated to a local funeral home.

With the death of Robert Personett, the local papers in northwestern Montana began to note in their coverage of boating accidents whether the victims were wearing life jackets. Personett and his comrades were not, and neither was Sally Boughner, a twenty-two-year-old visitor from Mason, Michigan, whose "kayak-type craft" capsized in the thirty-five-foot-deep water in a gorge on McDonald Creek, on the afternoon of July 30, 1971. Her companion, twenty-seven-year-old Murdock Hughes, scrambled his way to shore and ran for Avalanche Campground to get help, but Boughner did not emerge from the river. Members of the North Valley Rescue Association recovered her body the following day. "Neither of the two were wearing life jackets," the *Montana Standard* reported, a pointed warning to boaters in the park's treacherous waters to take this simple precaution to save their own lives.

In the curious case of the death of Perihan North, however, it's hard to say if a life jacket would have made the difference. North was the wife of a seasonal naturalist at Glacier National Park; her body was found in just four feet of water near the shore of St. Mary Lake on July 5, 1972, a short distance from her beached rubber raft. "The oars were in place on the raft, said [Chief Ranger Ruben] Har[t], and it contained a life jacket, purse, and partially eaten lunch," the *Montana Standard* said the following day. No further mention of this case appeared in print, so we will never know what actually took place to cause the young woman's death.

Equally mysterious is the case of James Krell, a forty-two-year-old Columbia Falls father of five who left his wife and kids at the Apgar picnic area on June 18, 1976, to take a final boat trip on Lake McDonald before leaving the park. Later that day, Krell's thirteen-foot aluminum boat turned up beached on the west shore of the lake, with "hull damage and a bent propeller," the *Montana Standard* reported. Searchers scoured the lakeshore for several days in hopes that Krell swam through the frigid waters to shore, but no trace of him ever came to light. To this day his remains are presumed to be somewhere in the lake.

CAUTIONARY TALES

Among the remaining stories of people losing their lives in Glacier's many waterways are some key messages for every reader of this book: Obey the warning signs; don't go into the wilderness alone; and don't believe for a moment that you are better, stronger, faster, or more nimble than the natural forces around you.

Mrs. Simon Olson of Moorehead, Minnesota, met an untimely end on June 3, 1941, for no good reason that anyone could determine. She and a party of relatives visited the park for a picnic along Avalanche Creek. Mrs. Olson asked her cousin, F. L. Figenskau, to take her picture while she sat on a log beside the creek. Figenskau took a few steps backward to set up the shot in his viewfinder, but when he looked again, Mrs. Olson was nowhere to be found. "He rushed to the bank just in time to see her swept into a narrow gorge with perpendicular walls," the Associated Press explained the following day. A rescue crew from the sheriff's office had to dynamite logs to free the body of the forty-eight-year-old woman from the gorge.

On a sunny July day in 1950, Frank A. Denney, manager of the State Theater in Cut Bank, went fishing in a boat on St. Mary Lake with a friend, Fred Mueller. They were out in the middle of the lake—a point where park rangers estimated that the water was about three hundred feet deep—when the weather changed so abruptly that neither man had time to take any precaution. Today's meteorologists call such a phenomenon a "microburst," a pop-up storm that sends rain, hail, lightning, and thunder into a concentrated area, and just as quickly ends, leaving a swath of highly localized disaster.

"The tornado-like wind came in from the southwest, roared through Kalispell, knocked down power poles, dislocated about 50 telephone lines and continued toward Hungry Horse Dam," the *Daily Inter Lake* reported the next day. "After approximately 20 minutes the wind disappeared almost as quickly as it arrived." The local weather bureau clocked this rogue wind at fifty-five miles per hour, with gusts of sixty-three miles per hour increasing its force.

And what a force! A motorist in the area counted twenty-four trees that had toppled into streets and come down on top of buildings. Windows in Flathead and Kalispell shattered with the abrupt change in air pressure, and roofs tore off of buildings like pop-tops on soup cans. In the forests, lightning touchdowns ignited fires in eight different places, keeping rangers and smoke jumpers busy throughout the night and into the following morning.

Amid all of this chaos and enveloped in gale-force winds and high waves, Frank Denney and Fred Mueller barely stood a chance of coming out of the storm alive. The storm tossed their small craft and batted it belly-up in an instant, dumping both men into deep water and deadly chop.

Somehow, against what seemed insurmountable odds, Fred Mueller managed to swim to the lakeshore and save his own life. Frank Denney was not so lucky, however. By the time the freak storm subsided and the lake had regained its normally glassy surface, Denney had vanished into its turquoise depths, quickly succumbing to the combined forces of bitter cold water and unmanageable waves. Searchers would never find his body.

Perhaps because they grow up in proximity to Glacier National Park and achieve an easy familiarity with its stunning but harsh landscapes, local residents are among the largest groups of people who meet their own deaths in the park. Dennis Brooks grew up in Whitefish and Hungry Horse, and when he came to visit his family from his home in Everett, Washington, he made a point of coming to Glacier National Park as soon as he had a few hours free. On November 21, 2005, Dennis and his sister, Denise Willis, and her husband, Cliff, came to the park and headed for McDonald Creek, stopping to enjoy the spectacle of McDonald Falls from the viewing platform off of Going-to-the-Sun Road.

Despite the warning signs that tell visitors of the slippery rocks and direct them to stay on the platform, Brooks leaped over the railing and began to hop from one rock to the next for a closer look. As he moved upward to the top of the falls, Brooks slid off the rocks and fell into the creek. His sister and brother-in-law watched helplessly as Brooks went over the falls.

"A little bit of moisture turns (those rocks) to grease," Chief Ranger Fred Vanhorn confirmed for the *Hungry Horse News* later that day. The paper's story continued: "The falls run through a torrent chute and then the creek largely flattens out not too far below them. People have fallen in the falls in the past and survived, riding all the way through the falls and the pool below."

Brooks, however, was not one of the lucky ones. The force of the falls pinned his body underwater in the twenty-one-foot-deep pool at its base. Divers rappelled down the gorge walls to reach the pool and recovered Brooks's body about three hours after he fell.

Bad luck also came to James R. Greene, a twenty-two-year-old former employee of Glacier Park Inc., the park's main concessioner, when he went canoeing on Swiftcurrent Lake in the middle of a July night in 2009 with his friend Joseph "Clay" Nelson. With air temperatures in the mid-forties at that hour, water temperatures must have been scarcely above freezing when the canoe capsized at about three a.m. Both men swam for shore and Nelson made it, but Greene succumbed to the cold water. It took twenty park employees to find Greene's body in the light of the following morning, in about eight feet of water some twenty feet from shore. What caused the canoe to capsize remains a mystery.

Equally mysterious is the case of Michael Sloan, sous chef at the Belton Chalet, who went out to Upper McDonald Creek on September 21, 2010, to fish in a spot where he had fished "probably a hundred times," according to his boss, Melissa Mangold, in an interview with the *Hungry Horse News*. Sloan knew the park's waters well because he fished nearly every day—and he usually took friends with him to share the pleasure of fishing in one of his favorite places. On this day, however, his friends could not break away to come with him. Sloan went fishing alone.

When he did not arrive for work later that day, the park began a search, finding his car in his usual preferred spot near the creek's upper bridge. His fishing pole turned up the next day, and divers took sonar equipment into the creek at its junction with McDonald Lake, where the pole was discovered. Two days of searching finally revealed Sloan's body about two hundred yards from shore, held down by the current at sixty-five feet.

To add another element to Sloan's inexplicable death, he was not wearing his chest waders. No waders turned up in the creek or the lake. "Something bizarre happened and no one knows what it was," Mangold said. "He knew there was a drop-off. He knew where it was."

DANGER IN SHALLOW WATER

Setting out alone into the Montana backcountry sounds entirely romantic and adventurous on its surface, but any park ranger will tell you that a solitary hike can end in disaster. When nineteen-year-old Jakson Kreiser of Hudsonville, Michigan, took a summer job at Lake McDonald Lodge in 2012, he could hardly wait for a day off to take on the Rocky Mountain wilderness on foot. Wearing a yellow sweatshirt and khakis and carrying a daypack, he strode off into the backcountry on Saturday, July 28, 2012 . . . and disappeared.

When he had not returned by nightfall, his friends notified park officials that Jakson had talked about hiking from Logan Pass to Avalanche Lake by way of Hidden Lake—a route for which there was no designated trail connecting the two lakes.

"The terrain includes cliffs with drops of more than 4,000 feet, wet and slippery boulders and dense vegetation," the Associated Press reported. His friends believed he planned to climb down some of the exposed rock faces on his intended route. Park staff found Jakson's car at the Logan Pass parking area, so they began their search along the route he had described to his friends. Park public information officer Denise Germann told the media that park staff believed that Jakson had very limited experience with backcountry hiking and that he might not be carrying much in the way of equipment.

Two canine teams, ground crews working throughout the night, aerial searchers using forward-looking infrared technology (known as FLIR) to detect heat sources, and people scanning the rock faces as the light changed throughout the day all became involved in the effort to find Kreiser. All of the area's rescue resources turned toward the task, from the trained trackers with North Valley Search and Rescue to the Flathead and Lake County Sheriff's Offices and the US Border Patrol.

On July 31 a ground crew found boot tracks near Mary Baker Lake that looked to be from Jakson's hiking shoes. The same day, a hiker who had been on the trail on July 28 called park officials, providing a credible description of Jakson and details on where he had seen the young man during his Saturday hike. Three days later another set of tracks led searchers into "a hazardous cliff band terrain," according to a park news release. "Four teams searched ledges and waterfalls in the Floral Park and Avalanche Basin areas, including a helicopter working in tandem with technical climbing teams. No signs of Kreiser were found."

After eight days of rigorous searching, there was still no sign of the young man from Michigan. The search entered a "limited mode" by August 6, according to a park news release. Jakson Kreiser's family issued a statement thanking all of the searchers for their efforts. "These men and women have been concerned, caring, courageous and amazingly compassionate in their search for our Jakson," they said.

Finally, on September 13, a pair of hikers happened across Kreiser's body in an area southwest of Hidden Lake, notifying park personnel at about twelve thirty p.m. of their find. Park rangers traveled to the site accompanied by the Flathead County coroner, and they quickly confirmed that the human remains discovered near Hidden Lake were those of Jakson Kreiser.

An autopsy revealed that Kreiser died of drowning and hypothermia, and the medical examiner judged that the young man had a serious mishap in very cold water. "Investigators believe he slipped while trying to cross a water course that essentially is created by snow field drainage," the MLive Ann Arbor website reported. "In late July, when Kreiser went missing, the drainage was likely 20–25 feet wide and up to 3 feet deep, with a temperature of about 36 degrees."

The website went on to note Flathead County deputy coroner Dick Sine's observations about what must have happened to Kreiser. "He said the water would have been rushing fast as well and, because of the cold, would be incapacitating to a fall victim very quickly."

Kreiser's family chose to see Jakson's last day in Glacier not so much for its final moments, but for the passion that led this young man to stride off into the wilderness on his own. "On a beautiful Montana morning, a rugged 19-year-old young man set off for a day hike to explore the mountains of his new summer home," his obituary in the *Lansing State Journal* read. "In this place Jakson found heaven with an endless view of snow-capped mountains, tumbling waterfalls and cool glacial lakes . . . In our hearts we are filled with the warmth of the morning sun that kissed our sweet boy's face as he walked happily along on his hike, marching to a tune of his own creation. We believe he was as happy as he had ever been as a grown young man."

CHAPTER 2

More Than the Heart Can Bear:
The Number-Two Cause of Death

IF A PERSON CAN BE PLEASED WITH THE MANNER AND LOCA-
tion of his death, then Dr. Frank Richard Oastler may well
have been content with his.

Dr. Oastler died quietly at Many Glacier Hotel on
August 2, 1936, from complications of a heart attack he had
suffered a month earlier on July 5. At sixty-five years old, he
had made the most of his remarkable life as a leader in the
field of gynecology, but he also devoted virtually every free
moment to furthering the cause of the National Park Service, especially when it came to Glacier National Park.

Oastler, a professor of surgery at Columbia University in
New York City from 1912 to 1932, and his wife—referred to by
park staff only as Mrs. Oastler—spent their summers exploring
the wilds of the American and Canadian west on horseback,
accompanied by a pack train of mules carrying supplies. They
made Glacier a stop on their tours nearly every summer, staying at Many Glacier Hotel during their periods of comparative
luxury before they rode out into the mountainous terrain.

Oastler documented their travels on black-and-white still and motion picture film, bringing home literally thousands of images and more than two hundred sixteen-millimeter films. All of this material now resides in the Yale Collection of Western Americana at the Beinecke Rare Book and Manuscript Library, which is located at Yale University in New Haven, Connecticut—but you can get a feel for the collection by visiting the library's website at http://beinecke .library.yale.edu/collections/highlights/frank-richard-oastler -home-movies and viewing four of the movie reels that have been restored for our viewing enjoyment. The seventeen-plus-minute movie of Glacier on the site features mule deer, mountain goats, bighorn sheep, and towering rock faces as the Oastlers and their pack mules made their way through a tricky mountain pass.

Park history credits Oastler with being the first Caucasian man to cross Surprise Pass, a backcountry route in the Coal Creek drainage above the Middle Fork of the Flathead River. Even beyond Glacier, Oastler is known for his instrumental role in saving the trumpeter swan from extinction, demonstrating his passion for bird conservation as a member of the American Ornithologists' Union. His photographs of trumpeters on their nests and in the wild broadened the conservation community's understanding of the factors that threatened these magnificent birds' survival.

Oastler built a vast collection of sixty-four hundred "lantern slides"—positive photo transparencies mounted for projection by a magic lantern, the slide projector that preceded the Kodak Ektagraphic carousel projector by about one hundred fifty years. As he shot his photos long before color film was invented, he colored them by hand to re-create the stunning landscapes and fascinating creatures he observed in the Montana backcountry. He traveled the country as a lecturer, teaching his audiences about the critical importance of conservation of this diverse landscape and so many others in the American west. Perhaps it was this function that led to his part in creating the National Park Service's public education program, as he demonstrated the role of knowledge and information in furthering the park service's goals of land and wildlife preservation.

So perhaps the good doctor found some contentment, or at least poetic justice, in spending his last days on earth in the national park that had served him so well for so many summers. Even after Oastler's death his wife continued to frequent the Many Glacier Hotel, arriving at the beginning of the season in a limousine and establishing a sort of residency in the hotel lobby. She continued this practice for twenty years after her husband's demise.

Chances are that activities Oastler undertook during his last visit to Glacier did not contribute measurably to his untimely death, as he was a seasoned outdoorsman who got plenty of exercise, even at high altitudes. We are looking at his death because Oastler is the highest profile of the forty-one known cases of heart attacks that ended visitors' lives in the park. In fact, heart events are the second-greatest cause of death in the park.

As most of these deaths never made the newspapers, it is difficult to say exactly why the majority of these people died when they did. We can gather some insights, however, from the medical facts about people with some form of heart disease visiting a park with the challenging climbs, major changes in altitude, and hundreds of thousands of backcountry acres we find in Glacier National Park.

Altitude and the Heart

If you've never traveled to a park or city at an altitude of more than 2,500 feet above sea level, you may not be aware of the difference in the very air that you breathe at this elevation. Here's what happens the higher up you go.

Starting at about 3,000 feet (914 meters), the air is literally thinner. Air closer to the ground is more densely packed than the air above it, because the weight of all that atmosphere presses down on the air—creating the "air pressure" you hear about during weather reports. The higher you go, the less atmosphere there is to press down on the earth, so the same amount of air is free to take up a larger space— making it literally thinner at higher altitudes. The air still contains the same percentage of oxygen, but it is spread out farther, so there is less oxygen in any given space. This doesn't make a lot of difference to your body at 3,000 feet, because your body generally takes in more oxygen than it needs and stores it for exactly this kind of eventuality. You may not even notice the difference, especially if you're riding in your car admiring scenery or if you get out only occasionally to walk to a viewpoint or follow a short trail.

If you're driving on Going-to-the-Sun Road from west to east, however, you will most likely begin your journey at Apgar Village Lodge, where the altitude is 3,166 feet (965 meters), and you will almost certainly stop at Logan Pass, where the altitude is 6,680 feet (2,036 meters). At Logan

Pass even the healthiest people will have some shortness of breath, especially if this is your first day at high altitude.

So if you're visiting from New York City, where you live at sea level, you may experience some discomfort—especially if, for example, you decide on your first day to hike from Logan Pass to Granite Park Chalet along the Highline Trail (about 7.5 miles each way, with an additional elevation gain of 1,920 feet). Your breathing will be more rapid as your body works to maximize the amount of oxygen it takes in, pumping it from the lungs into the bloodstream more quickly. You may feel your heart pounding as it works harder than normal to get more oxygen to your brain, organs, and muscles. As you start to exert yourself, you will become breathless, a sign that you are not taking in enough oxygen to fuel your lungs, heart, blood, and muscles. This breathlessness makes you slow down, which allows your lungs to catch up with the amount of oxygen your body demands.

If you've come from Denver or Albuquerque, however, you may feel much less discomfort, because you already live in a city at 5,000 feet or higher. You are used to breathing air with less oxygen content, so the effect may be very slight until you start climbing upward on a mountain trail.

People who have heart or lung conditions that affect their ability to process oxygen may feel breathless at higher altitudes even when they are not exerting themselves. This signals that the lungs may be developing a condition called high-altitude pulmonary edema (HAPE), in which fluid builds up in the lungs and keeps them from taking in enough air to refresh the oxygen supply. This does not happen in an instant—it can take several days at high altitude for HAPE to develop. Momentary breathlessness at Logan Pass is normal; continued breathlessness on your third or fourth day, especially when you are not moving around much, is a sign that you need to return to an altitude to which you are more accustomed. (You should also see a doctor if the condition does not correct itself once you reach denser air.)

You can avoid the discomforts of altitude changes by acclimating to the difference over the course of several days before you attempt a challenging hike or a bicycle tour of the park. National Jewish Health in the mile-high city of Denver, Colorado, one of the nation's top hospitals for people with respiratory, cardiac, immune, and related disorders, recommends these steps for all people traveling to a higher altitude than the one in which they live:

- Stay hydrated, and minimize alcohol consumption. Alcohol interferes with the blood's ability to absorb oxygen.

- Ascend slowly, and take breaks. Give your body the opportunity to adjust to the difference in the air pressure.

- Limit activity to a lower rate than at sea level, until you have been at altitude for several days.

- Raise sleeping altitude gradually. Many perfectly healthy people struggle with sleeping at a higher altitude. A rough night will affect your physical performance the next day.

- Stay conditioned and in shape. Before your trip, get into shape at your normal altitude, so exercising at the higher altitude will be easier.

So far, we've talked about people with healthy hearts and lungs. What about people who have active heart or lung disease? National Jewish Health has a number of recommendations for these patients, but for the most part, they all add up to this: Don't exercise at high altitude. If the condition is unstable—uncontrolled arrhythmia, decompensated heart failure, severe angina, or valve disease, for example—the hospital has just one recommendation: Don't go. "It may be good to postpone a trip until the heart conditions are stabilized, or avoid it altogether," the hospital's website suggests. "Always check with your doctor before any travel to high altitudes."

For the forty-one people who have died from heart attacks or other coronary events in Glacier National Park, this may have been the best advice. Just about all of these people passed away before Google made it easy to find these warnings, however, and some of them were young enough that they may have had no idea that they had a heart condition.

This may have been the case with Victor Seargent, who died at sixty in the park while on a driving tour with his wife, Irene. "While driving in Glacier National Park, he started to feel ill and suffered a fatal heart attack on July 10, 1958," his obituary tells us. Victor swam and rowed on the Schuylkill River in his native Pennsylvania in his younger days, and he was visiting Glacier from his home in Philadelphia—a city just 39 feet above sea level—when he died. Sadly, this may have been his first indication that he had a potentially dangerous heart condition.

The Glacier County coroner's report on the August 7, 1961, death of Gordon E. Scott, a forty-three-year-old man camping at St. Mary Campground with his wife and two sons, said that no inquest was required "as death was due to natural causes, probably a heart attack." Scott had been touring the park with his family, and died at three a.m. at their campsite (at an elevation of 4,488 feet). They came to Glacier from their home in Reedley, California, and we can only guess that Scott had a cardiac issue of which he was unaware until the night of his death.

Park records note that Rodney W. Long, who died of a heart attack in the park on August 23, 1969, was stricken while climbing that day. The *Daily Inter Lake* reported that the fifty-year-old man from New Hope, Minnesota, was camped with his wife and family at Fish Creek when the attack took place. In this case, as with the others, it's entirely likely that Long had no idea he had a heart condition until the moment when pain spread through his chest.

The moral of these and other stories in this chapter: Before you decide to travel to a place like Glacier at high altitude—a place where the magnificent scenery will make you want to challenge yourself by exploring beyond your usual activity level—check with your doctor to be sure your body can survive your adventurous plans.

IN TOP CONDITION

While a number of visitors to Glacier take on more athletic challenges than their cardiologists might recommend, some are not only in the right condition to hike at altitude, but they are also highly experienced at bagging Glacier's highest peaks. It turns out that top physical conditioning is no guarantee that hikers will come down from the mountains with their hearts and lungs intact.

At sixty-nine years old in 1988, Kalispell accountant Harry Isch knew his way around the tallest peaks in Glacier. He hiked regularly with the Thursday Mountain Club—also known as the Over the Hill Hiking Gang, a group whose members averaged sixty-five years of age and who had made as many as ninety hikes over the preceding three years, according to records kept by member Elmer Searles. Together the group enjoyed their favorite hikes up peaks including Painted Tepee, Altyn, Sinopah, Grinnell, Rising Wolf, Clements, and Siyeh, according to J. Gordon Edwards' book *A Climber's Guide to Glacier National Park*. "As anyone who has climbed here is aware, several of those peaks are NOT easily ascended!" the author notes. "To these senior citizens who are continuing to attain such lofty heights in Glacier National Park every younger climber must render deep respect."

When the group met to ascend Mount Cannon on July 21, 1988, their numbers included Isch, Dr. Harry Gibson, Pat Gyrion, George Ostrom, and six other hikers. They began their trek by hiking to the Hidden Lake overlook at Logan Pass and then continued around the northern tip of the lake to the trail up the mountain. As they began the ascent, Isch reported that he felt dizzy, and Dr. Gibson turned instantly to take Harry's pulse. Finding an erratic rhythm, he directed Isch to turn back, saying that he would accompany him to the trailhead. Pat Gyrion decided to come as well, just in case Isch needed more help.

On the way back they met a man from Gibson's office who took Isch's pack from him. "Isch turned to thank the man for carrying his pack, then collapsed," the *Hungry Horse*

News reported a few days later. "A passing hiker located a ranger who radioed for ALERT." ALERT stands for Advanced Life Support and Emergency Rescue Team, the area's medical helicopter transport service.

Three doctors and the ranger administered CPR, but they could not bring Isch back to consciousness. Ostrom later reported to author Edwards, "He made a joke just seconds before dropping; a peaceful death, with good friends, in a beautiful place."

A similar fate came to Henry Mayer, a celebrated biographer and historian whose book *All On Fire: William Lloyd Garrison and the Abolition of American Slavery* received high praise from *Publisher's Weekly,* the *Boston Globe,* and the *New York Times* when it was released in 1998. Mayer took a break from his work on a biography of photographer Dorothea Lange to visit Glacier National Park with his wife, Betsy, in the summer of 2000.

The Mayers selected a challenging trip offered by Backroads Bicycle Tours through the heart of Glacier, following Going-to-the-Sun Road to Many Glacier and turning north to travel to the adjacent Waterton Lakes National Park in Alberta, Canada. Fellow cyclist Robert Buffington, who happened to be on the same tour, describes the trip on his blog at http://buffpost.com/phlog/montana/, complete with dozens of photos that provide a delightful sampling of the views along the route.

Buffington provides what may be the only detailed description of what happened to Henry Mayer on this once-in-a-lifetime trip. "On the Going-to-the-Sun Road as we climbed towards Logan Pass at 6,680 feet, Henry suffered a heart attack," he reports. "Many of us were ahead of Henry as we wanted to get the big climb behind us, but news was trickling in from drivers who were passing us that there was a cyclist behind us who had a heart attack. This explained the numerous sirens you could hear in the distance . . . the sad truth was revealed when one of our leaders, Alexa, stopped to inform me that it was Henry who had the heart attack and that he died immediately . . ."

Buffington relates that he sat with Henry Mayer over breakfast at the lodge at Apgar that morning, before the tour set out on the ride to Logan Pass. "He was joking how he would listen in on the phone conversations with Betsy (an M.D. at Kaiser in Oakland) and her patients and try to figure out what the patient's afflictions were . . . Ironically, he indicated concern about the amount of cholesterol offered at the breakfast buffets at the lodges we were staying at. Of course, we just laughed it off and said it won't make much of a difference the next few days while we are riding 60 miles a day."

Liz Einbinder, spokesperson for Backroads in Berkeley, California, graciously returned my call asking if people die regularly on cycling tours of Glacier. She responded that in the staff's memory and in the company's records, no one else has ever met with such disaster on one of their tours. One death in a thirty-five-year history is a pretty good indication that most physically fit people will be safe bicycling through Glacier, as long as they take the time to acclimate to the high altitude.

CHAPTER 3

The Lure of High Peaks: Climbing Deaths

MOUNT JACKSON STANDS AS THE FOURTH-HIGHEST PEAK IN the Glacier National Park wilderness, covered in ice and snowfields and towering 10,142 feet (3,091 meters) above more than one hundred seventy other mountains in the park. Imposing enough on a warm July day when its sheer rock face juts high above the tree line, it intimidates even experienced climbers when snow shrouds its multifaceted surfaces in glistening white come November. By early January, Mount Jackson becomes encased in ice, and its height spurs its own microclimate, with whirling winds and blowing snow blotting out the magnificent view from its summit.

Why would anyone try to climb such a peak in the middle of winter? We can hear the famous quote to the media about Mount Everest by an exasperated George Mallory in 1924, "Because it is there!" These words, however, do not capture the climber's drive to take on greater and more daunting challenges, the constant testing of his or her physical abilities, or the lure that camping, climbing, and summiting in the grip of an icebound January may have for the most passionate seekers of adventure.

We can guess that this spirit and drive are what propelled twenty-year-old Kyle Borchert, twenty-two-year-old Shad O'Neel, and Taggert Schubert, who was twenty-five, into the Glacier wilderness on January 8, 1996, to summit Mount Jackson at the most demanding and desolate time of year. The three young men received a five-day backcountry permit from the park to take the Sperry Trail out to the mountain, listed their experience as "novice" in the climbers' register, and hiked out to take on one of the park's toughest climbs.

On the second day of their trek to the mountain, a storm pinned them down in place, forcing them to take cover at Lincoln Pass—one night in a tent and a second night in a snow cave, according to the report in the 1997 issue of *Accidents in North American Mountaineering*. Finally, on January 11, the weather broke long enough for them to relocate to Lake Ellen Wilson, where they established base camp for their climb on January 12.

They began their ascent at six thirty a.m., "equipped with technical climbing equipment and extensive bivouac gear," the report notes. "Borchert and O'Neel were wearing heavy climbing boots with 12-point crampons, while Schubert was wearing heavy pack boots with 4-point instep crampons. Each had an ice ax." Climbing essentially straight up from Gunsight Pass, they used snow pickets—strong anchors they drove into the snow and ice—all along their route to the summit.

They reached the summit at about two forty-five p.m. and decided not to linger there, as high winds pulled against their ropes and darkness came fast so soon after the winter solstice. For their route back to base camp, they chose to go down Northeast Ridge, which would be more sheltered from the wind and appeared to have a more gradual slope than the vertical route they'd taken from Gunsight Pass. Still, the wind yanked their rope, repeatedly forcing them off balance.

The three young men made the decision to continue their descent "unroped."

Borchert and O'Neel took the lead and moved ahead of Schubert, descending carefully and selecting only their next few steps as they went. They had traveled about two thousand feet when they stopped to consider the safest passage along several cliff bands that formed a sharp drop-off. Then they heard ominous sounds above them.

From about one hundred fifty feet away, Schubert had begun to fall. He glided past them in a blink, struggling desperately to self-arrest by planting his ax blade into the snow with his feet pointed downhill. Perhaps the ice would not give under the ax, or perhaps Schubert already had too much momentum to allow the ax to bite into the slippery surface. He could not stop his slide before he tumbled over the first of the cliff bands, falling about fifty feet to the next snowfield.

When he hit the ice the second time, Schubert no longer attempted to self-arrest. He slid down without resistance to another cliff band, toppled over that one as well, landed hard on the mountain's main snowfield, and slid even farther before finally coming to a stop some four hundred feet down the slope.

"Borchert and O'Neel descended rapidly to Schubert and found him to be alive but in grave condition," the report continued. "Schubert had suffered a fractured femur and was having difficulty breathing." Later a medical examination revealed broken ribs on both sides of Schubert's chest.

The two climbers worked quickly to dig a trench in the snow and make Schubert as comfortable as they could, and O'Neel began hiking out at three thirty p.m. to get help. Even in the middle of summer, this trek would involve a full day of strenuous hiking before reaching a phone or even a campsite. O'Neel made it in about nine and a half hours, making it to a phone just after midnight and calling park rangers for help.

Borchert, meanwhile, did everything he could to keep Schubert warm in the face of high winds and temperatures plummeting below zero degrees Fahrenheit. Finally, at about two thirty a.m., Schubert's battered body could no longer fight the cold. He died quietly, leaving Borchert to stay in place until a helicopter arrived at first light with emergency response equipment. Borchert, too, had begun to succumb to the freezing weather, and the rescue team treated him for hypothermia and frostbite in his extremities as he and Schubert were airlifted off the mountain.

Neither of the surviving climbers knew what chain of events had caused Schubert to fall, and even the author of the report (Glacier Search and Rescue Coordinator Charlie Logan) could only venture guesses based on his expert assessment of the circumstances on the mountain that day. "Contributing factors may have included Schubert's footwear used on wind slab and ice," he suggested. "The cumulative effects of fatigue, extreme cold and wind, haste, and dehydration may have contributed to diminished attention and caution at the initial, fateful moment."

He added at the close of his report, "While the climbers had some experience in winter mountaineering, none had ever attempted a winter ascent on a major peak. They had borrowed much of the technical equipment they carried and reported minimal training and experience in technical application. Schubert was the least experienced."

Beyond Experience, and Experience Beyond

As of this writing, thirty-four people have died in climbing accidents at Glacier National Park during the 102 years since the park began keeping death records. Considering the untold thousands of people who have climbed rock faces, bagged summit peaks, and conquered fields of boulders in this park, this is a very small number indeed—but closer examination reveals some interesting facts: Thirty of these deaths involved people in their late teens or twenties, and thirty-two of the people who died this way were male.

Rock and mountain climbing are largely male-dominated sports—in fact, reams of magazine articles and blog pages discuss this fact, although actual statistics are scarce. Those who engage in this sport tend to be on the young side, as flexibility is key to success and the human body loses this suppleness as we age. The ratios we see reflected in the deaths here in Glacier may well be comparable to the entire climbing community: 35 percent age nineteen and younger, 53 percent in their twenties, 12 percent over thirty, and a male/female percentage of 94 to 6.

These impersonal statistics do not really speak to the reality of climbers who have died in Glacier, however. In exploring their stories more thoroughly, we discover that most of the people who have lost their lives in this manner lacked the experience, the climbing equipment, or even the boots and clothing they needed to complete such a challenge successfully. Instead of putting in the time and effort it takes to learn the safest ways to enjoy this sport, many of these people simply walked out into the wilderness and started up a rock face, sometimes climbing with their bare hands. They didn't take the most basic precautions: climbing in a group; using anchors and a rope; or selecting the right shoes for traction before they began to scale a sheer wall of what climbers call "rotten rock," sedimentary rock loaded with cracks, fissures, and perpetually crumbling scree.

Take the case of Herbert Gray, a sixteen-year-old visitor to Glacier from Guilford, Maine, who left his aunt and uncle, Mr. and Mrs. D. P. Eldworth of Garden City, New York, at Granite Park Chalet on July 26, 1936, and went off to scale a sheer rock face along the trail to the chalet—a section known as the Garden Wall.

Today, the Garden Wall is one of the most popular sections of the Highline Trail from Logan Pass to the Granite Park Chalet, a 7.6-mile stretch of relatively flat trail (at least, compared with most other hiking trails in the park) that offers close-up encounters with bighorn sheep and mountain goats as well as some of the most spectacular mountain views in the park. It's a favorite with hikers, in part because of the unusual igneous rock formations the nearer the trail gets to the curiously named Granite Park Chalet. It is black basalt, not granite, which stands in pillow lava formations around the chalet area, creating a fascinating landscape that visitors will not see elsewhere in the park.

The trail runs along the Continental Divide, giving hikers one more reason to choose it during their stay at the park. High winds and wet weather are not unusual here, but a suddenly slick route can take hikers by surprise. A hiker wearing appropriate footwear with ankle support, carrying plenty of water, and bringing along an impermeable rain jacket and a fleece sweater will be ready for just about any eventuality.

Fleece clothing, Gore-Tex, and sturdy hiking boots were not available in 1936, however, so when Herbert Gray set out by himself not only to hike the Garden Wall but to scale it, he had only his hands and his wits to help him. The sport of rock climbing that is so popular in the 2000s had hardly even been considered this early in the twentieth century, so the gear that guides would recommend now would have been available only to serious mountain climbers. Young Herbert Gray certainly did not fit this description.

Gray never returned from his solo hike. After weeks of searching by trained rescue crews, park superintendent E. T. Scoyen told the Associated Press that he had "virtually abandoned hope" that Gray would ever be found. Searchers went down the rock face of the Garden Wall on ropes, but they could not find even a trace of the young man. "It is possible that Gray slipped and dislodged a heavy stone and was buried in a rock slide," Scoyen told the AP. "It is very doubtful he will be found alive."

Gray's body finally did turn up on August 12, eighteen days after he ventured out on his solo hike. He was found about a mile southeast of the Granite Park Chalet. "The youth apparently had fallen from a cliff and been killed instantly," the AP reported.

A similar circumstance—hiking and climbing alone— must have contributed to the death of Gilbert Shepard, a nineteen-year-old seasonal employee at Many Glacier Hotel, who fell from Mount Grinnell on June 20, 1938. No one knew the young man had fallen until searchers came across his body several days later. Records do not indicate what Shepard was wearing or if he had any kind of mountain climbing gear, but the fact that no one knew of his accident until they discovered his broken body tells us that he had ventured out into the wilderness unaccompanied and unprepared.

No climbing deaths were reported in the park for another twelve years, until July 12, 1950, when four boys from Tulsa, Oklahoma, chose an ascent of Mount Wilbur—a mountain that rises to 9,321 feet in the middle of the park's backcountry, and a total of 4,500 feet above nearby Swiftcurrent Lake. Often covered with snow year-round, this high peak poses a potential threat to even the most experienced ice and snow climbers. This group included John Fields, Chester Cadieux, Robert Stokes, and Dick Hughes, all in their late teens.

"When the group neared the top Stokes lost his footing and slipped on ice," the *Daily Inter Lake* reported. "He plunged about 200 feet into a narrow cavern and was believed killed instantly."

The other three young men in the party saw Stokes trying to work his way up a steep incline, but once he fell, they could not reach him. They left the mountain as quickly as they could to get help, reaching rangers that evening—but the rangers could not lead a search party into this treacherous terrain until the following morning. By noon they had located Stokes's body, tied ropes to it, and lowered it beyond the snow line to an area where they could carry it out.

"Rangers and trail crew men . . . said the boys were not equipped for mountain climbing on snow and ice," the Associated Press reported from West Glacier the following day.

What had the boys taken with them to prepare themselves for ice climbing? We will never know for certain, but the likelihood that they had any real mountain climbing equipment was low. Today, we have all manner of commercial outfitters to sell us any kind of gear we believe we will need, and experienced guides to show us how to use it and lead us up sheer rock faces covered with ice. In 1950, however, eighteen-year-old boys would not have the financial resources or the access to such equipment, or even the knowledge that they needed technical gear, unless one of them was lucky enough to have a parent who could supply it from his own stock.

Even more perplexing is the story of Robert Dion, a seventeen-year-old climber from St. Paul, Minnesota, who took on 9,541-foot-high Little Chief Mountain with two other boys, Bill Koch and Don Flynn, on July 29, 1952. Setting out from Black's Tourist Camp, the three boys had gotten part of the way up the mountain when Dion reached his limit for strenuous climbing. Rather than turn back or consider other options, Koch and Flynn decided to leave Dion where he was and continue to the top of the mountain. The spot where Dion remained was about a mile and a half above Virginia Falls.

"When they returned to the ledge, they found Dion's shirt," but no Dion, reported the *Daily Inter Lake*. "A search by the hikers revealed his body lying at the foot of a cliff. They estimated he had been dead several hours."

The surviving boys rushed back to their camp and found a ranger, and within hours a nine-person team headed by Chief Ranger Elmer Fladmark followed Bill Koch to the spot where he and Flynn had left Dion. The search party retrieved the body and brought it to the highway about noon the day after the accident.

It's certainly no surprise that boys in their late teens might exercise a lack of judgment, so the fact that these two hikers abandoned their companion on the side of a mountain simply becomes an example of unfortunate indiscretion. What happened next to Robert Dion remains a mystery. Did he fall asleep and slip over the ledge? Did he decide to try to follow his friends and lose his footing? Why did he remove his shirt? None of these questions were answered in the media of the time, but whichever mishap took place may well have been avoided if the hikers had stayed together. Word to the wise: If you must leave a comrade alone for a short time, take steps to be sure he or she is secure no matter what circumstances may occur.

One more case of a young man meeting an untimely death certainly warrants inclusion here, because of the national attention it attracted. On August 6, 1953, eighteen-year-old Peter Allen Kasen of Maplewood, New Jersey, set out to climb Mount Helen near Dawson Pass—a fairly short hike from Two Medicine Lake, and one that does not require technical gear—with three friends: Arthur Gold, who also came from Maplewood, and two brothers from Philadelphia, Morton and Barry Miller. They had chosen Mount Helen not so much to summit the 8,538-foot peak but because they had seen a snowfield on the opposite side that looked like a great place to slide down. At about five fifteen p.m., they had nearly reached the snowbank when Kasen slipped. He tumbled about fifty feet to a six-foot rock ledge and then fell over the ledge another fifty feet to land on rocks below. The final impact knocked him unconscious.

At first this story had the potential for a happy ending. Arthur Gold stayed with Kasen while the Miller brothers ran for help. It wasn't long before they came upon a trail crew camped nearby, who heard the boys' cries for help and radioed a park ranger to send a rescue crew right away. The boys were hopeful that their friend might survive this terrible accident.

District Park Ranger Paul Webb organized a rescue party, and they set off for the scene. Hours passed as the rescuers—reported to include twenty forest rangers and volunteers—traversed the distance to Dawson Pass from the nearest facility that had rescue equipment: "Rescue teams . . . arrived at the scene at about 10:45 p.m. after traveling four miles by road, four miles by water, two miles by trail and one mile over rough terrain," the *Daily Inter Lake* explained. "On the return trip, the rescue crew was met by a doctor who had been summoned from Glacier Park Hotel, who accompanied the boy to the foot of Two Medicine Lake, where the boy was transferred to a car at about 2:20 a.m. today and rushed to the Cut Bank Hospital." The hospital was another eighty miles distant. Eight hours later, and just four hours after finally arriving at the hospital, Peter Kasen died of his injuries.

This young man's death might have gone more or less unnoticed, but it attracted the attention of someone who could change the course of such rescue operations for the next unfortunate soul whose life might be in danger in the Two Medicine area.

In 1952, former First Lady Eleanor Roosevelt had spoken at Peter Kasen's high school in Maplewood, and Peter himself had the opportunity to provide the introduction of Mrs. Roosevelt to his classmates. Word of the boy's death reached the First Lady, and she addressed the tragedy in her "My Day" column, which was syndicated to newspapers nationally. She described her opportunity to meet him the previous year and the circumstances of his accident. "Because rescue equipment was not available, it was 12 hours before a force of 20 Forest Rangers and volunteers was able to carry him up the ravine," she wrote. "He was rushed to a hospital 80 miles away, but he died four hours later."

Peter's school planned a scholarship in his honor, she noted, but something had to be done in the park as well. "There is no doubt that in our national parks where climbing is done all the equipment that the National Park Service can afford to furnish is available. Appropriations, however, are never too generous and the extra help to provide even better equipment will be much appreciated in Glacier National Park, just as it would be in our other national parks," she said. "Tragedies such as this are harder to accept because we need our fine young people so badly. Of course, losing one of their classmates has made the students of this particular school and the people of this particular neighborhood conscious of the needs at Glacier National Park, but I can well imagine that there are other people whose youngsters will want to climb in Yellowstone or Yosemite and who also might want to be sure that not only the ordinary equipment but the best possible equipment is available in case of need for rescue work."

Whether Mrs. Roosevelt's influence made the difference or the park managed to get funding from another source, the availability and sophistication of rescue equipment improved significantly over the course of the next several decades.

EMPLOYEE DANGER

Earlier in this chapter we discussed some of the percentages that provide insights about the people who lose their lives in climbing accidents in the park, but here's one that reveals something alarming: More than 40 percent of the people who fall to their deaths are employed in the park at the time. Most of these are young people, working for one of the concessionaires as summer help waiting or clearing tables, cleaning hotel rooms, selling items in the gift shops, or otherwise earning money toward their college education while working in one of the most beautiful places in the world.

These young adults come from all over the country to work in the national parks. If you've ever visited one of the big park lodges or enjoyed a meal in a lodge dining room, you know something about them: They are well trained to offer you hospitality and a slice of their own backgrounds, chatting with you about their own experiences in the park while asking about your own. Many of them are eager to tell you about their studies at universities or their plans for graduate school and careers. These energetic young people are selected as much for their friendliness and sense of adventure as for their ability as servers or maintenance people, so they can make themselves part of the pleasure of visiting a national park.

So when one of these young men and women meets an untimely end at Glacier National Park, it raises questions. Aren't these kids warned of the dangers of venturing into the backcountry? Isn't anyone explaining to them that they need proper gear, footwear, and companions, and that they should not take on more challenge than they can handle? Hasn't anyone told them about the bears? How could such a thing happen?

The simple answer to this is, "Yes, of course." John G. Slater, a summer employee at the Glacier Park Lodge and the Many Glacier Hotel in the 1960s, described his own experience of this in a Glacier Park Foundation newsletter in 2000. He said he "had viewed the film 'The Mountains Don't Care' that Mr. Tippet had showed us in the employee orientation session. The film pointed out the various dangers that could befall us. However, the attitude that came with my age was that I was bulletproof, and I found it inconceivable that anything would happen to me." Slater goes on to describe a harrowing climb of Mount Clements that scared him enough that he acknowledged his own mortality, perhaps for the first time in his life. Luckily, he lived to tell the tale—but some did not.

The long-standing commitment to warning summer employees about the dangers of the wilderness must not have made its mark on three college students barely out of their teens in the summer of 1955, when they left the established trail and made an ill-advised climb up Altyn Peak.

Mary Jensen and Dell Beauchine, both from Minnesota, and a girl the Inter Lake News Service described as "pretty

June Johnson" of Euclid, Ohio, all took jobs at the Many Glacier Hotel that summer. On a day off they chose a 7,936-foot mountain peak to climb, perhaps because it was one of the closest mountains to the hotel, and one with a far less intimidating height than the tallest peaks in the park. They may not have taken into consideration the comparative difficulty of this specific mountain: The hike involves a climb up a precipitous cirque, a steep bowl shape with high walls on three sides, carved by glaciers many thousands of years ago.

Of the three students Johnson had the most hiking and climbing experience, but in this particular instance she was not in the lead. Perhaps she did not expect such a challenging climb, for none of the hikers had any kind of technical equipment with them. Details suggest that they believed they were out on a simple day hike and would be back at the hotel long before dark. On Altyn Peak, however, "visitors in the park were discouraged from climbing without adequate equipment and until they had consulted with park rangers," the news service reported the next day. These three hikers had not connected with the park staff before they chose this climbing excursion.

Captivated by the nature of a climb up high walls of rock, the hikers left the trail and headed up as vertically as they could manage. Suddenly Mary and Dell heard June scream. They turned back just in time to see her slip away down the mountainside and watched her fall more than a thousand feet to slam against the rocks below.

Mary and Dell turned back immediately and made their way to the hotel as quickly as they could. A search party of four people—park ranger John Higgins, Glacier naturalist

Don Robinson, and Glacier Park Hotel Company employees Art Kvelstad and Ronald Connor—set out at once to the mountain and began a fruitless search for June's body. Just as the three hikers had lacked proper equipment, so did these would-be rescuers—they had no way to find June's body at the bottom of the cliff.

At daybreak, as five fully equipped searchers arrived, the first group located the body. It took a third party with proper equipment for rappelling and carrying to finally remove June Johnson from the mountain. She became one of the first summer employees to die in a climbing accident at the park—but she would be far from the last.

In June 1961, seventeen-year-old James F. Moylan, a seasonal worker at Swiftcurrent cabin camp who had just arrived from Fort Wayne, Indiana, lost his life on Mount Henkel when he and his hiking companion, Douglas Krougher of St. Paul, Minnesota, strayed off the trail onto a steep slope of outcrop rock shale. Both boys slid over the cliff on loose shale, hitting the rocks below. Krougher's injuries were not fatal, but he could not walk after landing, so he continued to monitor Moylan's condition from a short distance away until a twenty-person rescue party found them both the next morning. Krougher reported that he saw Moylan get up and stagger around for several hours among the rocks, but he finally dropped to the ground and did not move again.

The stories of climbing accidents involving employees continue through the 1970s. John P. Hunting of Cedar Rapids, Iowa, took on a technical climb through Stoney Indian Pass in the northeastern corner of the park, accompanied by three other employees, Bruce Harvey, Ken Fielder, and Linda

Linkbiener. The quartet planned to take on the summit of Mount Cleveland, the park's highest peak at 10,448 feet, so they left early Sunday morning, August 18, 1974, to hike there through rough country. Properly equipped and not without experience, the group worked their way through Stoney Indian Pass at 9,500 feet until Hunting reached for a boulder and felt the sickening sense of empty air below him as the handhold gave way. He crashed down onto a snowfield and could not self-arrest, either because he had no ice axe or, more likely, because he could not turn his body to use it. The snowfield carried him to the edge of a cliff and dumped him over it.

The following July nineteen-year-old Gregory Finley from Sacramento, California, hiking with his friend Paul Ekness, slipped and somersaulted down a rock slope near Snyder Lake on the way back from climbing Mount Brown. Ekness moved quickly to reach Finley, but the boy was unconscious and could not be revived. Another party of hikers close by did their best to help, but Finley had internal injuries that kept him from regaining consciousness. The situation became even more complex when a rescue helicopter, dispatched to bring Finley's body out of the park, hit a tree branch with one rotor blade and had to pull back, leaving rangers no choice but to drop into the site from the air. Eight hours later a team of rescuers on horseback brought Finley's body out of the backcountry.

Reports about five climbers who took on the south face of Mount Siyeh in July 1976 do not tell us if they were equipped to make this technical climb. Just looking at the sheer peak, however—the fifth-highest in the park at 10,014 feet—tells even the novice that this is not a hike that can be attempted without some skill and prior experience. Today, the climbing website Summitpost.org notes a 4,200-foot vertical gain on the south slope from the Siyeh Bend trail to the summit, over five miles of hiking and climbing—"only about half of which is on trail." *Siyeh*, a Blackfoot word, means "rabid or mad animal," a further indication of the difficulty of this climb.

The party included David Boos, a seventeen-year-old worker at the Rising Sun Restaurant in the park who came to Glacier from New Hampton, Iowa. He and the other four people making the trek were already on the south slope by nine thirty a.m. when Boos simply fell off. Higher up than at least one of his companions, Boos hit Al Henning on the head as he fell. Henning, luckily, did not lose his grip on the rock wall.

When Boos hit the ground three hundred feet below, he did not move again. The *Independent Record* reported that the boy died before rescuers could reach him, but this did not stop Ranger Lloyd Kortge and Fire Control Aide Curtis Buchholtz from using the best possible gear to remove the body from its position at the bottom of a cliff. The team "lowered Boos's body 500 feet with a special cable rescue winch, then another 600 feet by ropes to the bottom of a series of cliffs," the paper reported.

After this accident summer workers seemed to take more care on their hikes and climbs for a time. Margaret W. Squibb, an eighteen-year-old woman working in the park in 1978, lost her life on a climb up Rising Wolf Mountain. In 1981, H. J. Donaghey, who was twenty-three, attempted a climb of Mount Stimson toward the end of the summer and fell to his death. Thor Tangvold, a 1985 employee, was barely in the park for a few days before he died in a climbing accident at Ptarmigan Falls on June 10.

In 1997, two seasonal workers—both well known to park staff as "knowledgeable and very experienced climbers and mountaineers," in the words of park spokesperson Amy Vanderbilt to the Associated Press—went off to make a one-day climb on the north face of Rainbow Peak. They wore crampons on their boots and carried ice axes, and while they were not roped together, they were otherwise prepared for whatever they would encounter during their climb.

Mark Robison and Chris Foster, both twenty-four years old and both natives of nearby Montana towns, left Thursday morning, July 3, 1997, to hike the steep, snow-covered chimney in Glacier's northwestern corner. They would reach the peak at 9,891 feet, which was well below the highest point in the park.

When the two men did not return by Friday morning, their coworkers reported their absence to the park's rangers, and a rescue team began the search. Saturday morning the team discovered the two bodies not far from the summit. An examination of the area did not yield many clues, though there was evidence of a rockslide nearby.

The park took advantage of the opportunity to warn visitors as well as park employees that while Glacier had a long reputation as a climbing destination, park staff did not condone the activity. "We do not recommend rock climbing in Glacier National Park due to the unstable and very dangerous nature of the rock found in this region," Vanderbilt told the Associated Press. "It is predominantly sedimentary, not mainly the granite you find in the Tetons. Footing can be precarious."

History to that date certainly bore her words out, so perhaps they had an effect; for a while after this, the frequency of deadly climbing accidents slowed, especially among summer staff members. Then early on the morning of Monday, August 29, 2011, park dispatch received a call from the supervisor of Jacob "Jake" Rigby, a twenty-seven-year-old seasonal employee from Illinois who was working with the park's exotic plant team, to say that Rigby had not returned from a personal day hike somewhere in the park. Rigby had not said exactly where he planned to hike on Sunday, but rangers checking the trailheads on Monday morning quickly located his vehicle at the Fielding trailhead on US 2 in the southern end of the park, near the Snow Slip Inn.

This discovery narrowed the park's search considerably. Rigby was a strong hiker and climber, so perhaps he had chosen an extreme mountain traverse in the area of Soldier Mountain, Sheep Mountain, Brave Dog Mountain, Mount Despair, or Eagle Ribs Mountain. Working to cover as much ground as possible in the shortest amount of time in hopes that Rigby would be found alive, the park dedicated more than fifty people to the search. Personnel from Flathead National Forest and Flathead Valley Search and Rescue assisted, bringing in a search dog team and people who had special training in tracking human beings. One thing Rigby's friends knew about him: While he had well-developed hiking and tracking skills, he also loved to hike off-trail. He could be virtually anywhere in the area.

By the evening of August 30, rangers had found a signature in a trail register that seemed to match Rigby's handwriting. It appeared that he had signed the summit register at Brave Dog Mountain, a route the park's communications described as "extremely steep and treacherous. It is an area that only the most highly skilled hikers and climbers attempt to access," the park's news release said. Rangers and rescue personnel planned to begin the following morning with an aerial search, while search crews bedded down in the backcountry so they could penetrate farther the following day.

On Wednesday, September 1, search crews reached the trail register on a mountain with no name, one locals and climbers knew as "8888," because it was 8,888 feet high. The weather-beaten trail register was empty, but "the lack of a signature is not considered clear evidence for Rigby's presence or absence from the area," the park's Wednesday night update release noted. 8888 is between Brave Dog Mountain and Mount Despair, in one of the most rugged and challenging areas of the park.

In rain and cold, search crews camped overnight on Wednesday and hunkered down again on Thursday in the area near 8888. By the time they reached 6,400 feet on Thursday afternoon, snow was falling—a bad sign for Rigby's potential survival.

Finally, on Friday, September 2, on the north side of 8888, aerial searchers hovering above the mountain discovered Rigby's body. It appeared that he had fallen some eight hundred feet from a ledge or rock face on the steep climb to the summit.

It took a specialized alpine recovery team from Waterton Lakes National Park in Canada, pilots and aircraft from Minuteman Aviation, and crews from the US Forest Service, Parks Canada, and Glacier National Park to remove Rigby's body from such a remote and perilous location, as well as the skills of the aviation staff at Flathead National Forest and Flathead Valley Search and Rescue. Together they brought Jake Rigby home to his family, who issued a statement thanking everyone involved in the rescue operation for their "dedication, support and professionalism."

THE SUMMER OF 2013

After two years with no climbing accidents among park concessions staff, two took place in the space of sixteen days in July 2013.

Cesar Flores, a cook at Many Glacier Hotel who had just completed his degree in culinary arts at Johnson & Wales University in North Miami, Florida, went out for a challenging day hike with three coworkers at seven forty-five a.m. They were headed to Apikuni Mountain, a rugged area with many cliffs and uneven terrain.

By eleven fifteen that morning Flores was dead, killed in a thousand-foot fall off one of the mountain's cliffs. His fellow hikers alerted the park staff as quickly as they could, saying that he was not responding to any attempts at communication and that they could not see his body. Aerial crews found it later that day, lowering a Parks Canada rescuer on a rope into the narrow area where Flores fell so he could assist in bringing out the body.

After Flores's death rangers redoubled their efforts to discourage summer employees from taking hikes that led off-trail into areas too dangerous for first-time or even intermediate hikers. Ranger Jennifer Lutman told NBC Montana that summer workers are told, "Make sure you're equipped with the right equipment, you're experienced, and you're hiking with others who are experienced as well."

Yet any parent knows that explaining the possibility of serious injury or worse to a young person in his or her late teens or early twenties produces nothing but rolling eyes and patronizing looks. Rangers' warnings often elicit the same kinds of reactions. Nonetheless, supervisors make every effort to impress upon summer employees that Glacier has a wide range of unique hazards: snow bridges that conceal crevasses in the ice, snowfields coated with slick ice, steep trails littered with loose scree, ledges that can give way underfoot, and wind-created slabs of snow that can break free and become deadly avalanches. Warnings often go unheeded, however, in the face of peer pressure to take on challenges beyond a summer employee's level of experience.

So when Matthew Needham and two other summer employees headed out to Grinnell Point for a climb on their day off, it's likely that none of them took the very real threat to life and limb very seriously, even though their fellow worker had died a little more than two weeks earlier. Needham, a twenty-one-year-old college student from Simi Valley, California, started working his way ahead of his friends on the trail. None of them could say exactly what made him fall, but suddenly he was in the air and gone, at the bottom of a sixty-foot drop.

This time another group of eight hikers came upon the body and were able to direct rangers to it, so a helicopter team airlifted Needham's remains out of the park that afternoon. The incident came to a swift end, though its impact remained with the summer employees for the rest of the summer. In all, five people lost their lives in Glacier National Park in 2013, making this one of the most dramatic seasons since the avalanche of 1969 (see chapter 7) and the gruesome Night of the Grizzlies in 1967 (see chapter 6).

WHEN VISITORS FALL

Not all climbing deaths in Glacier National Park happen to park concessions staff. When park visitors perish on their way up to a peak or—more often—on their way down, they are often inexperienced in climbing rock faces with the slippery, ice-covered, unstable ledges climbers are warned to expect at Glacier.

This was the case with former North Cascades National Park ranger Sam Raider, who fell to his death on July 3, 1976, while climbing Mount Clements. While we might expect a ranger from the land of high-elevation granite mountains to know what it would take to scale a sheer rock face, Raider's experience came from an area where the mountains are made of much more stable stuff than the mudstone shale, limestone, and dolomite walls in Glacier. Raider lost his footing and fell about three hundred feet to a snowfield, and then slid another six hundred feet before coming to his last resting place. Park spokesperson Dick Munro told the media that no climbing ropes "were involved as far as we can tell. He was climbing up the sheer rock wall alone."

In August 1971, thirty-two-year-old Ronald Matthews, a Big Mountain ski instructor from Whitefish, hiked from Lake McDonald to Sperry Chalet on a sunny Saturday with his wife, Andrea, and their four-year-old daughter, Sarah. On Sunday morning Matthews left his family at the chalet and joined three friends in hiking four miles to the top of Sperry Glacier, the park's largest glacier at three hundred acres, with the intention of skiing down the snowy slope. In the blink of an eye, Matthews lost his footing near the edge of a forty-foot crevasse and fell into the four-foot-wide crack in the ice.

Two friends stayed with Matthews while the third, Edmund Ray, ran back to the chalet for help. Soon a helicopter arrived on the glacier with men and rescue equipment to begin the work of pulling Matthews out of the crevasse. Pilot Bob Schellinger continued to ferry rescuers and equipment to the scene throughout the day until eleven men were in and around the crevasse, working against the clock to free Matthews from its icy grip. "The recovery operation required lowering a rescue team with a litter by ropes to the bottom, then hoisting the recovery party to the top of the ice rim," the *Daily Inter Lake* reported the following day.

Despite the fast response and the efforts of so many rescue personnel, Matthews sustained head injuries that were too severe to withstand the ordeal. By the time he reached the surface of the glacier at around six p.m., he had already died. "Rescuers thought there were signs of life when they reached Matthews but he was dead when his body was removed," the paper reported.

Matthews' death reminds us that even the most experienced hikers and climbers can find themselves up against conditions they did not expect.

Steve Fernekes and Ken Lynch, both in their late twenties, found themselves underequipped for the climb they undertook on October 12, 1983, a fall day that virtually guaranteed some ice and snow buildup on the rock faces they planned to scale. They took on the north face of Swiftcurrent Peak Glacier and apparently made it to the top without incident—but like so many climbers detailed in this chapter, they found the way down to be more hazardous than they expected. "Fernekes had climbed down to a ledge," a report in *Accidents in North American Mountaineering* described. "Lynch handed down some equipment and was attempting to climb down to the ledge. Fernekes was holding Lynch's foot in a small crack. Lynch lost his hold, fell approximately six meters, and was stopped by rock. Fernekes fell and slipped off the ledge and down the rock face about 180 meters, landing in the bergschrund," a crevasse created between a moving glacier and a wall of stationary ice.

Analysis of the accident indicated that ice on the rocks was covered in snow, masking the ice and making conditions "extremely hazardous" for climbing. After days of intermittent rain and snow, the rock face received no direct sunlight, and the temperatures, just above freezing, were not enough to melt away the slippery surfaces. All of this makes it clear that it was the wrong day to scale this face, but the report had one additional observation: "These climbers did not have crampons, ropes, helmets, hardware, or adequate clothing, and had little experience."

The park's records include the name of another climber who lost his footing while heading down one of Glacier's highest peaks. Roger Dokken, climbing Mount Cleveland with three friends on September 1, 1997, fell behind the two leaders and made the final scramble to the top of the highest mountain in the park with Marvin Parker, a hiker with similar skills. They stopped to enjoy the views from the summit before following two other hiking companions, Jim Egan and Vern Ingraham, who had reached the peak earlier and were already heading down to their camp at Lake Mokowanis. Dokken and Parker took the ridge south of Mount Cleveland along the Stoney Indian Peaks. Egan wrote in a trip report on the County Highpointers Association website at cohp.org: "This is a class 3 route with incredible scenery and unforgiving exposure along the ledges which are generally several feet wide, but have loose scree in spots and thousands of feet of air below if you should stumble while you take in the sights."

Egan and Ingraham were well ahead when Parker and Dokken started down, and they made it back to their camp and spent a leisurely evening waiting for the others to join them. By morning, however, when Parker and Dokken had not appeared, they suddenly became aware that a helicopter was searching along the route they had taken the day before. Certain that one of their fellow hikers was injured and the other had been able to go for help, they made their way back to the trailhead and their vehicle as quickly as they could. Sure enough, rangers had left them a note asking them to contact the nearest ranger station right away. Rangers were ready to break the news: Roger Dokken had lost his footing and fallen thousands of feet to his death.

"Marvin later recalled how they had reached the summit and that the wind had died while they were enjoying the incredible views," Egan wrote. "They had started back with plenty of time to reach the trail before dark, and Roger was elated to have reached this mighty summit. He died doing something he enjoyed tremendously."

CHAPTER 4

Racing to the Sun:
Motor Vehicle Accidents

By all accounts, Richard "Dick" Fish could not have been a more accomplished motorcycle rider. The tribute to him on the All Harley Drag Racing Association (AHDRA) website noted that he may have led the membership—as well as that of the long-distance-riding Iron Butt Association—in the number of miles he logged on a motorcycle in his seventy-year lifetime. Fish once spent twenty-one days riding from the very top of the continent in Prudhoe Bay, Alaska, all the way to Ushuaia, Argentina, where the road ends at the southern tip of South America.

With that challenge under his belt, Fish established the route for another ride from Prudhoe Bay—this time to San Lucas, Mexico, then across the continent to Key West, Florida, and up the east coast to Goose Bay, Labrador, finally coming to an end in central Colorado. "Fittingly, the ride has become known as the Ultimate North American Insanity," the tribute says.

A dirt bike rider, a mechanic, a commercial pilot with Air Canada, and at one time a bison rancher in his home province of Alberta, Canada, Fish made himself a pillar of the motorcycle community. He promoted AHDRA races, rode thousands of miles to attend and participate in events, and even repaired other riders' bikes and other equipment before big rallies. To his fellow riders Dick Fish seemed an indestructible force, one that would be part of their experience for many years to come.

It was absolutely inexplicable, then, that Fish would bobble a curve on Going-to-the-Sun Road just east of the Avalanche parking area at five thirty p.m. on a summer Saturday, skid into an oncoming vehicle, and get thrown from his motorcycle.

The details that came later made the accident even more unbelievable. No one was speeding in either direction. The rally had just started, so Fish was alert and most likely enjoying a fairly easy ride. No animal had rushed into the road, so Fish was not swerving to avoid a bighorn sheep or a Columbian ground squirrel.

A second's distraction, perhaps, or a tiny fault in judgment was the best guess anyone had about what the investigating officer would call a "freak accident." Whatever the cause, the result was the same: Fish fell from his bike into the path of the oncoming car. While his helmet remained securely in place, he died of trauma to the head, apparently sustained when the car ran over him. "Once on the ground Fish could not avoid the oncoming vehicle," the local newspaper the *Missoulan* reported.

As with so many vehicle accidents, the investigation revealed no definitive cause. No other casualties were reported, however, and an hour or so later, law enforcement and emergency crews had cleared the road and sightseeing resumed on this sunny Saturday, July 23, 2011, on one of the world's most spectacular roadways.

DYING TO SEE THE PARK

If you have ever driven the fifty-mile Going-to-the-Sun Road (Sun Road for short), the two-lane highway that traverses the heart of Glacier National Park, you have almost certainly wondered whether all those other drivers enjoying it with you understand how precarious a route this extraordinary highway can be. Not only does it provide the breath-stealing thrill of sudden drop-offs just past the guardrails, steep walls of rock rising for hundreds of feet above your sunroof, and undulating curves that bring you close to the edge, but it seeks to distract you with some of the most extravagant scenery you will see from your car anywhere in the country.

How can you keep your eyes on the road when there's so much to see? The park provides many pull-offs to allow you to stop and savor the fantastic sights around you, with the goal of helping you watch where you're going whenever your car or motorcycle is in motion. Stopping is not only encouraged, it is preferable—the adventure of driving this road is in taking it slowly.

As stunningly beautiful as it is, Going-to-the-Sun Road can be precarious. People have indeed lost their lives driving its length—though perhaps not as many as you might assume. Since the first sections of the road opened in 1933 (the rest were completed by 1937), only eight motor vehicle accidents on this road have resulted in deaths. (There also have been two suicides, which you will read about in chapter

10, and several other accidents involving people who left their cars and fell over an edge. You'll find more about these in chapters 5 and 13.)

The first recorded death on this road came to thirty-four-year-old Lloyd Campbell on August 24, 1937, although the date and name are the only details available. Not until August 3, 1986, did the park note a second motor vehicle death here, at the Weeping Wall—an area where six to eight former underground streams cascade over the rock wall, first exposed by blasting during Sun Road's construction back in the 1930s. It's hard to say exactly why Ross Reed lost control of his vehicle there in the peak of a dry summer, when the waterfalls would have been little more than a series of sparkling trickles, but the park records his death with no further details.

In June 1987, motorcyclist Bradley Cox lost his life near Triple Arches, and three years later, in August 1990, Norman J. Wiebe also had a fatal motorcycle accident on this same stretch of road. While plenty of caution signs warn of the hazards at Triple Arches, not all drivers and cyclists follow the instructions to slow down and watch the road carefully through this area. Winter and early spring rockslides and avalanches are common along this particular section of Sun Road, and these dramatic events have broken off chunks of guardrail, making the passage risky for drivers who do not follow the instructions on numerous warning signs. In the early 2000s, the park completed a major restoration in the Triple Arches area by installing steel-backed guardrails that can be removed each fall to allow avalanches to pass through without further damaging these protective barriers.

Most motor vehicle accidents in the park barely make the newspapers, because they are the result of life taking its own course—someone losing consciousness behind the wheel through a heart attack or other natural cause—or a split-second error in judgment. A tragic event in 2004, however, highlights the hazards people devise of their own volition simply by taking unnecessary chances.

On Friday, September 3, 2004, a Ford Explorer careened around the hairpin turn at the Loop, near the Sun Road's midpoint north of Granite Park and the Weeping Wall. Inside the speeding car were nineteen-year-old Simon Chavez; Joseph Burdeau, who was twenty-three; and two minors who were not named in the media. The nineteen-year-old driver of the car, East Glacier resident Angel Star Makescoldweather, had had more alcohol than logic would dictate before driving this precarious road—and in a critical moment she missed the opportunity to turn the wheel and sent the vehicle flying into the air, plummeting in seconds to slam into the rocks below. The Explorer rolled another one hundred to one hundred fifty feet, finally coming to rest on its roof.

The passengers were not wearing seat belts, so when the Explorer rolled, they were thrown from the vehicle. "Two were in a ravine and not immediately visible," the *Hungry Horse News* reported.

There's no record of how exactly the park staff heard about the accident, though the impact may have been loud enough to grab the attention of staff members at Logan Pass. Two rangers were on the scene in short order, climbing down to the victims and receiving medical supplies from a third rescuer, who came down using rope and other equipment.

It took twenty-five park personnel, including ten to twelve rangers, to carry out the rescue. "Park rangers were able to get the victims back up to the highway where they were transported by ambulance to locations on the Sun Road where the ALERT helicopter could pick them up," Chris Peterson of the *Hungry Horse News* reported. The structural fire brigade came from West Glacier to help, and a private nurse who happened to be in the area came to assist as well.

Thanks to this remarkable rescue operation, all five victims were airlifted from the Sun Road and taken to two hospitals for emergency treatment. Four of these young people survived, but the driver, Angel Makescoldweather, died from her injuries later that night. It would be well into the fall before park staff and contractors could remove the wrecked vehicle from the area, closing this portion of Sun Road while they did so.

Five years passed before the Sun Road produced its next fatality, this time a motorcyclist from Okotoks, Alberta, Canada. George Stephen Zlatnik was one of twenty-seven riders traveling as a group, driving east on the road between Logan Pass and St. Mary. When the motorcyclist just in front of Zlatnik looked in his rearview mirror, he realized that he could no longer see him. He moved quickly to alert others, but by the time rangers discovered Zlatnik and his Honda Goldwing lying thirty feet below the road about half a mile west of the Wild Goose Island overlook, he was already dead from the fall. Investigators concluded that the rider simply failed to negotiate a turn, and while his helmet remained securely in place, he died from other injuries.

THE EARLY DAYS OF DRIVING

There are other roads in Glacier National Park, of course, some of which have been there since before the park was dedicated in 1910. On these roads early accidents took place at slow speeds between motorists driving their first-ever vehicles, often without much regard for the safe driving rules barely outlined by state governments. In 1935, as the Civilian Conservation Corps worked to build new roads in our national parks, only thirty-nine states required drivers to obtain licenses to operate a vehicle—and few of these states required applicants to take any kind of a driving test. With a growing number of cars on the road being driven by people with little training, even the nation's most unpopulated areas—like this remote corner of northwestern Montana—would undoubtedly experience the tragedy of motor vehicle deaths.

Fifteen-year-old Geraldine Bogar, from Spokane, Washington, was on her way to a picnic with several other passengers in a car driven by Ralph Drury, seventeen, from nearby Belton, Montana, where Geraldine was visiting her uncle. When Drury rounded a curve about half a mile south of Fish Creek Campground, where the CCC contingent working in Glacier had made camp, he swerved a bit into the center of the road. He did not see the CCC truck driven by Robert Mack coming toward him at the crushing speed of eighteen miles per hour until the two vehicles were very close to one another. At that moment Drury and Mack both swung hard to the right, avoiding a head-on collision that might have killed them both. Mack's truck struck Drury's car just behind the rear door, where Geraldine Bogar happened to be sitting.

The impact threw Bogar forward, striking her head on a doorpost. In the seconds following impact, Drury did not know that anyone in the car had been hurt, so he swung across the ditch alongside the road and brought the car back onto the highway. Only then did his other passengers—his sister, Evelyn Drury, and friends Isabelle DeVall and Chester Mahoney—alert him that Geraldine was slumped forward and bleeding. Rescuers rushed Geraldine to the hospital in Kalispell, but her head injuries proved to be too severe and she died half an hour after she got there.

Ralph Drury was quick to tell officers that he was driving safely on the right side of the road when the truck cut a corner and crashed into him. The other CCC employees in the truck, however, said the truck was also on the correct side of the road and was traveling at under twenty miles per hour when Drury's car sped around the curve. They said they saw Drury attempt to turn out of the way, but the impact of the collision tore the rear end off his sedan.

The county coroner moved quickly and ordered an inquest to take place the following day to determine if any charges should be filed against the drivers. He assembled a jury and held the inquest in the park, taking the jury members to the scene of the accident and reassembling the evidence. He had both cars returned to their exact positions at the moment of impact. Witnesses to the accident also participated, telling the jury exactly what they saw in the seconds before and during the crash.

It took the jury less than an hour to determine that carelessness and negligence on the part of each of the drivers led to Geraldine Bogar's death. If this led to some kind of punishment, however, the newspapers of the time did not record it.

The media did note that eighty people had died on roadways throughout America over that July 4 weekend in 1935, nearly as many deaths as we experience today on a holiday weekend—but there were only 23 million cars on the road back then, while the auto industry research firm IHS tells us that we have 253 million cars on the road in the United States today.

A Series of Bizarre Circumstances

Most motor vehicle accidents in Glacier National Park involve strange events that the driver may have been powerless to avoid. Take, for example, the sad case of nineteen-year-old Charles Norris, who was on his way to Whitefish on his motorcycle on a dark Saturday night in July 1951 when a horse with no rider suddenly charged out in front of him. Unable to pull up short, Norris struck the horse and was thrown from his bike, dying at the scene. The horse also did not survive the incident.

John Jam, a twenty-six-year-old Kalispell man completing his college degree at Montana State University after serving his country for three years in Korea, drove through Many Glacier on the night of August 21, 1955, and somehow managed to flip his car over a cliff. He plunged down one hundred feet, but the car landed on its wheels and, remarkably, seemed able to continue, so when a passing motorist stopped and found Jam unhurt, he said he would go for help—and he took Jam's ignition key with him, clearly to keep him from getting back on the road. Jam, however, was one step ahead of this good and wise Samaritan. He produced a second key and drove away . . . and drove off the highway again about sixty feet later, rolling down another cliff and ending his life. Whether this death was actually Jam's intention will never be known.

Leo Bowman became one of ten Montanans killed on Memorial Day weekend in 1959—though the only one in Glacier—when his motorcycle flipped on a rough patch of road two miles north of Babb on the road to Many Glacier. His eleven-year-old son, Leroy, was riding on the back of the bike, but rescuers rushed him to a hospital in Alberta, Canada, and he survived the accident.

A few weeks later the chief electrician for Glacier National Park, James D. Grist, died in a head-on collision with Robert D. Lynch, an aluminum siding salesman from Great Falls. Lynch, who also died in the crash, was reported to be driving on the wrong side of the road when he collided with Grist. County Coroner Sol Catron reported to the media that Lynch's car "'folded up' after turning end over end three times when it plunged off the embankment." Grist, meanwhile, was found "pinned beneath his car with head and body fractures when highway patrolmen arrived after the accident was reported at about 5 p.m." Both Lynch and Grist were dead by the time emergency services reached them. Three passengers in the two cars were taken to Kalispell General Hospital and treated for injuries, but they all survived the accident.

In the summer of 1968, a car containing four seasonal employees of the park's concessionaires spun out of control on the Many Glacier entry road and careened through small timber and brush on its way to Sherburne Lake. Before the car reached the water, it rolled, shaking all of its passengers and throwing nineteen-year-old Diane Neale from the car. Neale landed in the water, but not before the car rolled over her, causing head and neck injuries that became the cause of her death. The Glacier community waited to hear what the coroner's inquest would reveal about the cause of the accident, but no sooner had Coroner Bill Riddle impaneled a jury to examine the case than he suddenly canceled the inquest altogether. "Glacier County Attorney Dan Welch could see no necessity for an inquest," the *Daily Inter Lake* reported several weeks later, even though it also noted that Riddle had started down the track to begin a formal inquiry. No more about the incident appeared in the local papers, so we can only guess what may have transpired in the weeks between the accident and the attorney's decision not to examine the case any further.

On an icy December day in 1970, seventy-two-year-old Roscoe M. Perry, a retired automobile dealer from Lake Blaine, drove his pickup truck on US 2 east of Goat Lick at a few minutes before noon. He hit a patch of ice and began to spin, sliding off the downhill side of the highway and plunging 168 feet before the truck made its first impact. With so much momentum, the truck kept moving, becoming airborne for 56 feet while it plummeted to the top of the next cliff. It toppled end over end for another 100 feet, finally finding a landing place on a sandbar in the Middle Fork River, another 30 feet from the base of the cliff.

We know all of this because a passing truck driver, logger Keith Engle of Kalispell, stopped when he saw the pickup begin to slide and watched it fall over the cliffs. When the pickup finally came to rest and Engle could see nothing moving, he flagged down a bus on its way into the park and reported the incident to the driver, Tom Landis, who continued into the park and stopped at the first place with a phone. At the Snow Slip Inn, he called the Columbia Falls Police, who were at the site in minutes.

When the police saw the wreckage, they put the word out to the Flathead Lifesaving and Rescue Association that divers and emergency equipment would be required. In the meantime, a police officer started down the fifty-degree slope himself, reaching Perry after carefully picking his way along the cliffs to the battered pickup. He removed Perry's body from the cab of the truck and assisted as the Flathead rescuers sent down a sled and a long cable, bringing the sled and the body back up by winch. The process took three hours, including recovery of the pickup—which turned out to have minimal damage considering that the driver inside did not survive the fall.

Traffic fatalities in the park by this time were only a tiny fraction of those across the county and the state—and the newspapers in the area had become fairly obsessed with totaling up the figures year after year. Coverage of Perry's accident announced to readers that his death brought the total fatalities from auto accidents for 1970 up to twenty, putting the county "within three deaths of the all-time traffic fatality record established in 1967."

The toll continued to mount through the 1970s. Maynard Kitzman, a fifty-five-year-old man from Minot, North Dakota, wrapped his car around a tree east of Many Glacier during the July 4 weekend of 1971, one of six fatalities across the state that weekend—bringing that year's total to 129. During July 4 weekend in 1974, motorcycle rider Roy Chrissman, a boy of eighteen, ran into an oncoming car on US 2 west of Goat Lick. Young Coleen Griggs lost her life in St. Mary in 1979 in a motorcycle accident, and Carla McLean died in a car near Two Medicine in 1981.

When a tractor-trailer rig jackknifed near the Watson Ranger Station in July 1984, the resulting accident killed passenger Robert Wayne Herron, a thirty-four-year-old man from Hungry Horse. But this year the accumulated death toll across the state began to drop, hitting 134 by July 23, 1984—16 fewer deaths than the year before.

Indeed, the motor vehicle casualties became fewer in the park as well. A year with more than one death was rare, and some years saw no fatalities at all. Perhaps the many new safety features developed during the 1980s, 1990s, and 2000s have reduced the number of incidents, or maybe the thrills of speed and recklessness are not what they used to be, especially for visitors to national parks. Whatever the reason, fewer people are dying in their cars and on their motorcycles in Glacier National Park—and that's good news for everyone.

CHAPTER 5

Know Your Limits:
Hiking Accidents

By all accounts, Yi-Jien Hwa had an uncommon enthusiasm for backpacking in the roughest American wilderness. Born in Malaysia and a graduate student at Asbury Theological Seminary in Wilmore, Kentucky, twenty-seven-year-old Hwa maintained a blog on the equipment review website backpackgeartest.org, where he wrote extensively about his experiences with various kinds of gear and his plans for trekking through the Glacier National Park backcountry.

Hwa had started backpacking as a teenager, but his self-professed obsession with the sport came to him around 2007, when he wrote in detail about the kinds of hikes he wanted to attempt. He and his wife, Siu Yin, planned to embark together on the most ambitious hike to date: a ninety-six-mile trek across Glacier that would begin at St. Mary, cross some of the park's most treacherous terrain south of Logan Pass, and then head north in the direction of Kintla Lake Campground. The route would take eight days to complete, a challenge even for the most spirited and experienced mountain climbers.

Shortly before they were scheduled to begin this trip in the summer of 2008, a family emergency forced Siu Yin to forgo her participation. Hwa had two options: He could postpone the trip until his wife could accompany him—after months of planning, auditioning gear, stocking up on supplies, and selecting the timing to coincide with Glacier's most navigable season—or he could set out on his own. He chose to go solo.

When Hwa arrived at the park and visited St. Mary Visitor Center for a backcountry permit, he described his itinerary to the rangers there. Beginning at Logan Pass, where he would leave his vehicle for the duration of the trek, he would begin with a lengthy hike to Sperry Campground, which would take him off-trail as he passed through Floral Park and the Sperry Glacier basin. On his second day he would head for Reynolds Creek Campground, northwest of St. Mary Lake, and stop at Logan Pass to pick up the supplies he stored in his car. His third night would be spent at the Granite Park Campground, more than seven miles from Logan Pass, and then he chose 50 Mountain Campground at the Continental Divide for his fourth night. Kootenai Lakes was his fifth-night destination, and a day's hiking from there would take him to Hole in the Wall Campground. Hwa planned to reach the Upper Kintla Lake Campground on his sixth night and continue north from there to the Kintla Lake trailhead, a final hike of 11.6 miles. He would finish his remarkable tour of the park on August 18.

The rangers at St. Mary tried to talk him out of the trip, but Hwa was determined to take on this monumental challenge. They finally issued him the permit, but with a long list of warnings about all the things that could curtail his adventure: hypothermia, bears, mountain lions, waterborne pathogens like giardia, a staggering elevation gain and loss of 14,000 feet, snow, rushing water, and the strong likelihood of severe weather.

"We have no desire to deny people access to their own park," Ranger and Incident Commander Patrick Suddath told blogger Eric Newhouse, whose extensive analysis of Hwa's hike can be found at http://glaciernationalparkhiking .blogspot.com/2008/09/anatomy-of-lost-hiker.html. "Although we give advice, we have to rely on good internal judgment."

Park spokeswoman Norma Sosa spoke with Newhouse in early September 2008 as well. "Even for a seasoned mountaineer, this is an extremely hard and dangerous itinerary," she said. "The biggest red flag was that he was a solo hiker. This is not a hike we would advise to attempt solo."

Every day of this experience would present its own challenges, but some of the toughest would come on the first day as Hwa approached and then descended into Floral Park. A wildflower-covered series of grassy slopes in spring, this segment of the route from Logan Pass to Sperry Chalet follows the comparatively easy Hidden Lake Trail for three miles, skirts the southern shoulder of Bearhat Mountain, and then climbs above the lake and almost immediately drops into a basin. Crossing the basin leads to a gentle route up to the surprise revelation: Sperry Glacier, and an expansive view of the route to come on the way to Comeau Pass. A short distance to the right, hikers reach the top of a high ridge with a view of Avalanche Lake some four thousand feet below.

From here the downhill route to Mary Baker Lake leads, at last, into Floral Park.

This devilishly vertical hike involves enough changes in elevation to discourage hikers who are out for a casual stroll or a day hike, so the chances of Hwa meeting anyone at all during his first day out were very slim indeed. To make the day even more challenging, Floral Park would not be a final destination in what was already a lengthy, taxing hike. Hwa's plan called for him to reach Sperry Campground, which required several miles of rugged, obstacle-strewn hiking beyond the wildflower meadows. While the area has more scenery in a condensed area than you might find in other entire states, it's also packed with boulder-strewn trails, snowfields, glacial crevasses, ice-cold streams, many stretches where the trail becomes indistinct, high ridges, slopes covered with loose scree, steep descents, and any number of tricky passages.

What exactly happened to Hwa as he traversed these trails, scree fields, and game paths will never be known—but more than a week later, when his wife and mother alerted rangers that Hwa had not called them on the appointed day to tell them he was at Kintla Lake Campground, the route to Floral Park was the first area that rescue crews began to search.

How did they narrow the search so quickly? Hwa's car remained at Logan Pass, fully loaded with the supplies he had planned to pick up after his second night in the wild. He never circled back to Logan Pass. Search crews tracked down every hiker to whom they had issued a backcountry pass to the Sperry Campground, and no one remembered meeting a solo hiker. Hwa apparently ran into serious trouble on his first day in the wilderness.

By the time his family knew that he had not returned, he had already been missing for a week.

Where could he be? Hwa could have fallen into a crack in the earth or in a snowfield, slid down an ice chute until he was concealed by overgrowth, sunk to the bottom of a lake, or been swept away by a stream. He might have crawled into a hole or under an overhang for shelter, making him invisible to helicopters searching for his body. Any fall from a cliff might have brought enough loose rock down on him to hide him from view.

"By month's end, searchers logged more than 2,500 man-hours looking for Hwa," Newhouse wrote in his blog on the incident. "Thirty to 60 searchers were shuttled in and out of remote areas by helicopter and horse-mounted patrols were used, as were human-scent dog teams and aerial heat-sensing equipment. Suddath estimated that the searchers eliminated 90 percent of the options Hwa could possibly have chosen."

Eight people from Flathead County's mountain rescue team came in by helicopter, equipped with advanced gear that allowed them to explore crevasses in Sperry Glacier. Some team members actually descended into the cracks to search further, while others on the team probed the crevasses that were wide enough to allow a visual inspection. No human footprints were visible on the glacier's surface, in part because three inches of new snow had fallen since the day Hwa might have passed through the area.

As no clues came to light, however, the park had no choice but to start scaling back the search. On the seventh day just two search teams continued on the ground in the park, including one fifteen-member team with technical rope training, who focused on Sperry Glacier and the surrounding area.

"We are still hopeful that additional information will eventually surface that will lead us to Yi-Jien," Suddath told reporters on August 26. "But we know that the odds for that outcome are reduced with each day that goes by. In the absence of a promising development, we will be scaling back the operation." Two teams continued their efforts for another week, but when no additional clues came to light, they, too, ran out of options. The park made the difficult decision to end the full-scale search, though they made a commitment to Hwa's family that they would continue to look into new leads and analyze any evidence that came to light, no matter how far in the future that might be.

Three years later—on July 3, 2011—hiker John Wagner and his grown son, Christopher, started an ascent of the headwall of Avalanche Lake as a possible route to Floral Park. The route didn't pan out, but as they climbed a dry creek bed on the east side of the lake's headwall, John saw something he did not expect. He got closer and found the bits of color he spotted in the weeds to be a nylon strap and a pair of long underwear. "He thought it odd that someone would leave or even lose clothing in a gully at this remote location," the *Hungry Horse News* noted, "so he reported his find to Park rangers."

The find recharged the search. Wagner directed rangers back to the spot where he found the clothing, and rangers gathered additional evidence, including bone fragments from the long-decomposed body. They found pieces of equipment that Hwa detailed on his equipment list when he applied for his backcountry permit. "Rangers believe the evidence was transported down slope from the cliffs above by water and snow avalanches," wrote *Hungry Horse News* reporter Chris Peterson.

The park sent the bone fragments to the National Missing Persons Program at the University of North Texas Center for Human Identification, where they were examined over the course of several months. On May 31, 2012, the anticipated announcement came that closed the case: The bone fragments and clothing were indeed the remains of Yi-Jien Hwa.

In a follow-up article a few days later, Peterson noted, "With just bone fragment remains and a few tattered clothes, it's impossible to tell the exact cause of death."

The saga of Yi-Jien Hwa, an enthusiastic young man with a passion for the outdoors, ended in the worst possible way—and with a great deal of heartache for his friends and family as the years dragged on with no clues to his disappearance. Now, with his story finally concluded as much as it can be, we still don't know what went wrong. We can, however, take one lesson away with us for our own explorations of wild places.

Rule Number One: *Don't hike alone.*

The Unscheduled Fall

The vast majority of people who hike at Glacier National Park and all the other parks in the National Park Service come home alive and unscathed, and nothing in this chapter is meant to discourage you from setting out into the wilderness for your own adventure. That being said, it's critically important that you take all the logical precautions when going out on walkabout in unfamiliar territory, no matter how carefully you have planned and how much protective clothing, gear, and equipment you carry.

You may be thinking that you would never take on a challenge the likes of the one planned by Yi-Jien Hwa, but the fact is that most of the hikers in Glacier who do experience fatal accidents are not nearly so extreme. All too many of these, in fact, are people who climb over guardrails or barriers to have a closer encounter with nature or who step too close to a wilderness feature to enjoy it safely.

WATERFALL DEATHS

What is it about waterfalls that attract so many people to risk their lives by coming closer? There's an industry around this in upstate New York, where thousands of people don bright-colored ponchos and board the *Maid of the Mist* boat rides daily to come close enough to Niagara Falls to get drenched in its torrential downpour. Falling water hypnotizes and mesmerizes onlookers, it beckons us to come closer and be cleansed in its showers, and it offers cooling refreshment when its force remains gentle and tropically warm. In Glacier National Park, however, waterfalls maintain a temperature of about thirty-six degrees Fahrenheit and fall with the power of millions of gallons of snow meltwater from May until well into August.

These threats to life and limb do not become apparent to visitors until they thrust a hand into icy water to sense just how close to freezing it actually is. For some visitors the moment of truth comes an instant too late.

In July 1960, Frederick Robert Steinmetz, an eighteen-year-old from Detroit, Michigan, working a summer job at the Swiftcurrent Motor Inn, stopped on his hike in Red Gap Pass to drink from the top of a waterfall. It's understandable that he would need a drink, and that he might not have carried enough water if he did not realize how strenuous a hike this would be: Red Gap Pass involves a rise of more than fifteen hundred vertical feet in 2.5 miles, a tough go for even the most experienced hikers. The waterfall stop proved to be the wrong choice, however. Steinmetz's hiking companion, Tom Linnerooth, watched as his friend lost his balance, slid over the crest of the falls, and tumbled to the bottom one hundred feet below. It took Linnerooth several hours of frenzied hiking to reach park rangers who could help, but by that time, Steinmetz was long since lost.

Many years later, in the summer of 1998 and in just about the same spot, twenty-seven-year-old Brian Donald-Nelson of Seattle met the same fate. While hiking with his wife and two other people, Donald-Nelson decided to attempt to get a drink from the stream above an unnamed waterfall southeast of Red Gap Pass. Just as they had for Steinmetz, the rocks proved too slippery for safety, and Donald-Nelson plunged into the water. He sailed over the falls and fell about one hundred fifty feet before he died on the rocks below. (Another hiker, trying to fill his water bottle, fell in the same place about a month later. While he suffered head injuries, he survived the accident thanks to a dramatic helicopter rescue.)

Barely a month later visitor Lillian Mayall of Moosejaw, Saskatchewan, Canada, lost her footing as she admired Lake McDonald Falls from a cliff above it and fell forward over the precipice into the falls. Young Loretta Wist, visiting the park with Mr. and Mrs. Mayall and their two sons, Donald and David, saw Lillian fall but could not tell if she had tripped, slipped, turned an ankle, or had some other mishap that sent her plummeting over the cliff. Whatever the cause, the result ended the fifty-two-year-old Mayall's life on what was supposed to be a pleasant holiday with her children.

July 25, 1964, began as a day off for Kenneth Gelston, a summer employee at the Rising Sun Motor Inn, and a female companion not identified by media. Gelston and his friend were spending their Saturday hiking in the St. Mary area when he stepped out on some of the rocks at the top of St. Mary Falls. Suddenly his feet went out from under him on the slippery rocks and he plunged into the water. The current took him over the falls between the rocks, dropping him twenty feet to the first landing and then another twenty-five feet down into the plunge pool at the base of the falls. The force of the water drove Gelston's body down into the deep, frigid St. Mary Lake. Flathead scuba divers searched for days in and around the falls, first removing fallen logs with snags of roots from the ledges to see if the young man's body was pinned underneath. They found no trace of Gelston, however, and whatever remains of him lingers in the lake to this day.

For the family of six-year-old Laura Jean VanMun of Kimberly, Wisconsin, the lure of a waterfall ended in unspeakable tragedy. On the first day of their planned two-week vacation in August 1965, the child, her father, and her two brothers climbed up the side of Trick Falls in the Two Medicine Area. Laura suddenly lost her footing, and before anyone could grab hold of her, she tumbled over the bank, landed hard on rocks, and fell into the water. Her family watched helplessly as the current took her over the ledge and down ninety feet into the pool below.

Two strangers who saw the accident managed to pull Laura out of the water at the base of the falls, where rangers moved quickly to administer oxygen. There was nothing they could do for her, however, and a doctor at the scene noted that she had probably died in the fall from the impact on the rocks.

The most difficult deaths to understand are those that result from a momentary lapse in judgment or an act of sheer foolishness. In August 1973, seventy-two-year-old Karl Staner, visiting the park from Albuquerque, New Mexico, so admired McDonald Falls that he felt the need to climb over the rock barrier—the wall put there for his safety—to get a better angle for a photograph. That snapshot cost him his life; he slipped, fell, and joined the cascading water over the Lower Falls. He emerged floating face down about fifty yards past the base of the falls, with wounds to his head that told the story of the beating he took on the way down.

TRIP, SLIP, AND FALL

This last group of fatal trail accidents includes the ones that make the least logical, rational sense: the sudden stumble, the ledge that gives way underfoot, and the meander past the boundary the park considers safe.

The Reverend Joseph H. Devaney, a Roman Catholic priest visiting from Fort Myers, Florida, met an untimely end on July 30, 1966, when he lost his footing on a slope of Mount Oberlin. The mountain, about a mile and a half from Logan Pass, is considered a "friendly" Glacier hike because it offers an easy ascent—at least, compared with the many peaks above 9,000 feet throughout the park. At 8,180 feet it takes less than half a day to climb from the visitor center at Logan Pass, and today the well-marked trails provide the simplest route through the landscape with the least potential damage to the fragile ecosystem between the visitor center and the peak. In 1966, however, it may have been easy for a hiker to lose his way a bit and end up in areas that require scrambling—and this may be what happened to Reverend Devaney. Another park visitor discovered him late that evening, with head injuries that led to "massive brain damage," according to the *Daily Inter Lake* the following day.

Here's where the story gets a little weird. Two weeks later and only about two miles down the road, another Roman Catholic priest met a similar end. Paul Schreiber, chancellor of the diocese of Dodge City, Kansas, parked his car just west of Logan Pass and got out with his traveling companion, Marlin L. Werner, to admire the view. In a split second Reverend Schreiber slipped on some gravel, lost his balance, and fell off a cliff, tumbling about a hundred feet to his death. This accident took place on August 13, 1966.

Another man of God passed away in the park in the same general area, but many years later. In 2001, Don Fogg Harris, a retired schoolteacher and an elder and missionary in the Church of Jesus Christ of Latter-day Saints, got out of his vehicle at the Crystal Point turnout and fell from there onto Going-to-the-Sun Road below. The fall, a simple foot fault, brought him swiftly to the end of his life in one of the most beautiful places on earth.

A similar fate came to William Labunetz, a sixty-seven-year-old neurologist from Great Falls, when he and four other hikers—including his thirty-eight-year-old son—were on the way back to Many Glacier Campground from the Helen Lake area in August 2009. Labunetz chose to take Ahern Pass, a route he had enjoyed on a previous visit, rather than continue on the easier path with the rest of his party. A few minutes after they separated, Labunetz plunged three hundred feet off the mountain to his death, in full view of another group of hikers. One of the hikers was a park employee, and he rushed to the point of impact to try to help. "The park employee found the neurologist had already died of major injuries," the *Flathead Beacon* reported the following day.

When Park Café summer employee Matthew Wiesike set out at four p.m. on August 5, 2002, to climb Reynolds Mountain alone, he seemed to have little understanding of the challenge he planned to undertake. While he had told some of his coworkers that he planned to climb this mountain—or perhaps another mountain like Heavy Runner or Bearhat—he did not share with anyone which mountain he had finally chosen before he set off. He carried water and a camera, but no food, tools, or supplies, making it highly unlikely that he would survive for long if he lost his way or sustained an injury—and establishing beyond a doubt that he had no idea how strenuous a hike he planned to undertake.

Wiesike did not even sign in at the Logan Pass Visitor Center, so he did not leave any kind of itinerary there to let rangers know his plans.

On Tuesday morning, when he did not report for work, his friends had little information to offer the rangers they contacted. Nonetheless, rangers began an extensive search, organizing thirty-five people to canvass the area on and around Reynolds Mountain. Two helicopters and three dog teams assisted on the first day, but low clouds made a thorough search of the mountain by air very difficult. When dawn came on Wednesday and the clouds lifted, however, one of the helicopter crews spotted the young man's body at the bottom of a cliff in the Hidden Lake basin just after nine a.m., far below the western face of the mountain. "According to rangers, Matthew Wiesike was ill-prepared for his climb and was not on the standard climbing route," the *Independent Record* reported. The young man from Orange Park, Florida, may not have had the basic trail-finding skills required in the northwestern Montana backcountry to keep to a well-traveled route.

Even people with the most developed backcountry skills can slip and fall, however, as did Nicholas Ryan, a former strength coach at the University of Nebraska and the owner of a fitness business in Omaha. Ryan took the Grinnell Glacier Trail from Many Glacier to Grinnell Lake, a generally flat route through stunning country, and then began the steep climb—aided by switchbacks—from there to Grinnell Glacier. "Park officials posted a 'snow hazard' sign at the trailhead on June 28, and travel on this trail is not advised," the *Hungry Horse News* reported. The signs went up several weeks before Ryan's trek—which was on July 18, 2011—warning hikers not to take this route because of a number of issues along the way: snow on the trail, steep snow bridges, and a waterfall that sprayed the trail and created icy surfaces. The trail would not be cleared of snow until the end of July.

Somewhere along this trail Ryan slipped. He fell two hundred eighty feet onto a snowfield and continued to slide, but the impact on snow, ice, and rock took his life long before his body came to rest at the end of the snowfield. His experience in the wild, his ability to endure physical challenge, and his level of preparedness for this trip could not save him from the most basic hazard: the slick, glossy sheen of ice on the trail. Worse, he ignored the warning signs, the classic mistake of the supremely confident.

In the summer of 2013, one of the deadliest on record for the park—though every case had its own story, and you'll find the others in chapters 3 and 12—a sixty-four-year-old visitor named Charles Fred Huseman also shrugged off the warning signs that told him the Highline Trail was still closed because of lingering snow at the end of June. Huseman slipped while crossing a snowfield just a mile west of Logan Pass in the Rim Rock area, fell about a hundred feet, and landed hard on Going-to-the-Sun Road. Because his fall took place in the middle of one of the park's busiest areas, many witnesses watched in horror as Huseman fell.

"An ice ax is essential equipment for hiking high slopes and passes early in the season," Rich Landers commented at the end of his blog on Huseman's death on the *Spokesman-Review*'s Outdoors page. Knowing how to use such a tool is also essential, and worth practicing on a well-contained snowfield before any trip into Glacier National Park.

The park's most recent falling death—and one of the most inexplicable—came in the final days of summer 2014, when a group of friends including eighteen-year-old Brandon Luis Avalos, a visitor from St. Maries, Idaho, made the drive along Going-to-the-Sun Road to Logan Pass sometime after sunset. They stopped at around ten p.m. on Thursday night, September 18, at the Big Drift area, and Brandon left the car to explore on his own while the others stayed close to the road. As the hour grew later, the friends waited for Brandon to come back, finally spending the night at Logan Pass with the thought that he would come back there to find them. When morning came and he had not returned, they left their vehicle to look for him.

They found Avalos about one hundred feet straight down from the road. He had climbed over the guardrail in a steep area in the dark, where many cliff bands crisscrossed the mountainside and huge rocks protruded from below. Chances are that, with the confidence and sense of immortality so many teenagers believe is their birthright, he simply took a step forward in the deep darkness of a wilderness night and met empty air. We can be thankful that his friends had the good sense to stay put overnight and not to try to find him in the dark—possibly forfeiting their own lives in the process.

TRIBUTES IN THE PARK

A final note: If you spend some time in Glacier, you may come across plaques in two places in the park, each noting the passing of young men who met their end while climbing Glacier's mountains. The one found at Logan Pass states,

"In loving memory of Dr. Charles Bauer, who met his Savior Jesus on his favorite mountain, Mt. Reynolds, in Glacier National Park." This one gives May 31, 1986, as the date of his accident. No further details seem to be available about this loss of life.

The other, found at the top of Mount Gould, honors Josh Skibsrud, "who fell while climbing Mount Gould's west face on July 19, 1992. He was 20 years old." I could find no more information on this young man either. Each of these tributes deserves mention, however; perhaps you will stop and give a moment of silence to these two men and their untimely endings at the literal height of their desire to explore.

CHAPTER 6

Bear Bait:
Grizzly Encounters

OF ALL THE WAYS PEOPLE MAY DIE IN ONE OF AMERICA'S national parks, few make a visitor's heart stutter in fear like the potential for an attack by a grizzly bear.

For more than fifty years in Glacier National Park's history, such attacks remained the stuff of paranoid imagination. The grizzly bear, the larger of the park's two bear species (the other is the black bear) and the largest mammal in North America, generally regards humans as something to avoid, lumbering away if people happen across it on a wilderness hike or drive up as it feeds on berries in the shrubs alongside a park road.

Grizzlies—so called because of the silver-gray frost that mingles with the many shades of brown in their fur, creating a "grizzled" appearance in sunlight—are fairly easy to tell apart from the smaller black bears also found in the park. The prominent hump on the bear's back just behind the head, the luxuriously thick brown coat, and the sloping forehead that gives the bear a "dished-in" look all provide onlookers with immediate clues to the bear's species. Spotting a grizzly in the wild has always been one of the top attractions of a visit to the park, though it's tougher in modern times to find one than it was in 1967, when the first story in this chapter takes place. Back then the bears regularly visited sources of human food, and park visitors could watch the huge animals plunder open trash dumps in central locations in the park.

Wait. What?

It's hard to imagine that the National Park Service, one of the nation's leaders in preserving open space and endangered species, once looked the other way when it came to feeding bears in the national parks. If you've visited Glacier National Park recently, you know that the park's literature warns against leaving food out that may attract bears, and that visitors are directed to dispose of waste in rugged, heavy, bear-proof trash receptacles. If you camp, you must keep your food in a bear-safe container, and rangers are ready to instruct you on the most effective methods for storing your food out of reach of bears. Even stopping your car along the roadside to view a bear has become a potentially hazardous situation, as bears that get used to cars also become habituated to the presence of human beings. The park's website notes, "Habituated bears may learn that it is acceptable to frequent campgrounds or picnic areas, where they may gain access to human food. When a bear obtains human food, a very dangerous situation is created that may lead to human injury and the bear's death."

The park learned the hard way that these warnings are necessary, in a time when people and bears had formed relationships that not only endangered the bears' survival but that had become deadly to humans as well.

A VERY QUICK HISTORY OF GRIZZLIES IN AMERICA

Long before Glacier became a park, as many as one hundred thousand grizzly bears wandered the western region of North America, finding plenty of habitat and more than enough sources of food. They dined on cow parsnip and glacier lily, huckleberries and raspberries, and other fruits and shoots throughout the growing season, and they plundered winter-killed carrion when snows fell. The only humans they encountered came from the occasional community of indigenous people who killed the odd bear for food and pelts but did not go out of their way to disrupt the bears' way of life.

The arrival of the Lewis and Clark expedition in 1805 brought the region and the enormous bears to the new Americans' awareness, as the explorers established a route for future settlement. After Lewis and Clark returned home and shared their vast knowledge with the easterners, the federal government took steps to open the new American west to settlers, and tens of thousands of people began to pour into bear country. New settlements brought farmers who turned vast areas of land to agricultural use; mercenaries and traders turned territories into towns and cities; and people began to fear for the safety of their livestock and children against the largest wild animals—especially the bears, which weighed in at nearly eight hundred pounds and measured more than seven feet tall when fully erect. Bear killings became a natural part of the new western way of life, with each trapping or shooting yielding a useful pelt and hundreds of pounds of good meat. By the end of the nineteenth century, the killing forced the grizzly population down to just a few thousand bears. (A great irony in this time came from California, where the state flag sports a grizzly bear, but the bear had been completely extirpated from California by the time the flag was adopted in 1911. The artist used the state's last bear in captivity as a model for the flag's illustration.)

Pushed out of most of their former habitat, grizzly bears congregated in the last remaining open spaces, including the land preserved by Yellowstone National Park's formation in 1872 and by the creation of Glacier National Park in 1910. For many years after the US Congress passed the act creating Glacier National Park, grizzly bears continued their accustomed way of life under the protection of the federal government, with one new element: They became an attraction, a much sought-after part of the wilderness experience.

With the construction of the interstate highway system in the 1950s and the onset of the road trip as the ultimate family vacation, people began to travel from across the country to America's national parks. The more these visitors clamored to see the bears, the more park management took steps to make it easier to see them.

"In the 1950s and '60s, the wilderness experience with bears had been diminished to mean feeding bears out of cars, bears appearing in front of spotlights and bleachers in Yellowstone, and in both parks, bears scavenging for food in garbage dumps," the PBS documentary *Night of the Grizzlies* tells us. As the popular 1960s television show *Walt Disney's Wonderful World of Color* brought the national parks into our living rooms on Sunday evenings, viewers had the pleasure of seeing bears coming right up to car windows in Yellowstone and Glacier to enjoy food scraps offered by visitors. At dusk dozens of bears gathered at open trash dumps at the parks' most popular campsites and feasted on the scraps they found there, to the delight of visitors who came to watch.

Park management at Yellowstone embraced the attraction by setting up bleachers so people could sit and watch black and grizzly bears at close range rooting through the garbage to find whatever delicacies had been left behind by careless campers. Archival footage found by *Night of the Grizzlies* filmmakers shows us a black bear standing up on its hind legs to beg for morsels from a visitor not three feet from the animal, and a bear digging through the spill of an overturned trash can, looking for the remains of visitors' dinners.

In Glacier much of this kind of activity took place at the Granite Park Chalet, an area reachable only at the end of a 7.5-mile hike from Logan Pass on the Highline Trail, along the Continental Divide. Young chalet manager Tom Walton, hired by the park in 1967, carried on the decades-old tradition that summer of putting out food scraps every evening to attract grizzlies. The bears put on quite an impromptu show for the hikers and campers who gathered to watch, fighting among themselves for a pound of bacon and other particularly desirable leavings.

"By early August, the Granite Park Chalet's official two-month season was half over, and the grizzlies' visits to the garbage dump had become a big talking point in the park," wrote *Sports Illustrated* writer Jack Olsen in his bestselling account, *Night of the Grizzlies*, on which the PBS documentary is based, "but the Park Service's public position was that animal feeding was strongly prohibited by several dozen rules and regulations, and therefore it must not be going on."

Despite all this proximity, potentially dangerous encounters between people and grizzlies had remained at a minimum. Hikers told stories of a bear charging them when they startled one in the wild—for all of its powerful build, the grizzly has poor eyesight and only average hearing, so it can be surprised easily by hikers—but most stories placed the bears well away from visitors, spotted by an observant hiker on the opposite side of a meadow or distantly through the trees in the park's dense forests. Bears rarely if ever approached humans, seeming to live up to the old adage, "They're more afraid of you than you are of them." While there had been reports of some injuries from bear attacks over the fifty-seven years since the park's formation, *Homo sapiens* and *Ursus arctos horribilis* seemed to coexist cautiously but comfortably, as long as each species maintained a respectful distance from the other.

All of this changed in the summer of 1967, culminating in a night that shattered any notion that grizzlies and humans could take their relationship for granted.

THE FIRST ATTACK

On Saturday, August 12, 1967, fires burned in locations throughout the park after a dramatic electrical storm ignited "smokes" the day before. More than one hundred lightning strikes had reached the park floor, setting ablaze parts of the forest that were parched from a particularly dry spring and summer. This did not deter hikers and campers from exploring other areas in the park, however, so the Granite Park Chalet fed a capacity crowd and entertained them at dusk with the five grizzly bears that frequented the open dump behind the building.

Many park personnel had visited the chalet that summer, and manager Tom Walton believed he'd received a tongue-in-cheek, wink-and-nudge kind of message from a number of them that he really should not be feeding the bears, but that they could see how much people certainly were enjoying the spectacle. To date, no one had reported a close encounter with a charging bear in the campgrounds near the chalet, so park staff and campers believed, as they always had to that point, that the bears were relatively harmless and disinterested in the humans who watched them.

This was not the case some twenty miles away in the campground at Trout Lake, however. Throughout the summer, campers had reported that a particularly unusual-looking grizzly bear, a thin one with a mangy coat and elongated head, came into campsites repeatedly and raided them for food. While bears often fed on scraps left behind by campers in sites throughout the park, this particular bear not only chewed its way into canned foods, but it tore up backpacks, sleeping bags, and tents in an apparent search for a more substantial meal. In July, John Cook and Steve Ashlock, two fourteen-year-old boys from a nearby town, had to cut their three-day camping trip short when this skinny bear ate most of their food and ripped through their packs and equipment, refusing to clear off even when the boys pelted it with small rocks. The *Hungry Horse News*, the area's weekly newspaper, reported that the boys were the "latest" to escape this bear and that queries the paper made to Glacier Park's rangers had gone unanswered.

Other Trout Lake campers had reported similar confrontations. A troop of six Girl Scouts and their leaders abandoned the site after a grizzly of the same description plundered their food and belongings, and a young couple on their honeymoon watched as the bear shredded their entire food supply and all of their camping gear. A number of hikers and overnighters left descriptions of the same kinds of experiences with this peculiar bear in the register at the trailhead at Lake McDonald. When the most agitated campers reported the incidents to rangers, wrote author Olsen in *Night of the Grizzlies*, they were met with amusement, unconcern, and even boredom. Was it possible that the rangers did not make the connection between all the frequent attacks? Given the busy season, record crowds, and the many small forest fires that caused road and campground closings throughout the summer, the rangers already had their hands full without the burden of organizing a bear hunt and removal.

So by the second weekend in August, when teenaged seasonal park employees Julie Helgeson and Roy Ducat chose Granite Park Chalet's campground for a wilderness overnight, they cheerfully told other campers in the vicinity that there was nothing to fear from the neighborhood bears. An Ohio native, Ducat was a sophomore majoring in biology at Bowling Green State University and working as a busboy for the summer at East Glacier Lodge. Helgeson, a sophomore at the University of Minnesota, met Roy while she worked in the laundry at the same lodge, and the two planned what would be Julie's first overnight wilderness hike. They hitchhiked to the Logan Pass trailhead and continued on foot along the Garden Wall to Granite Park Chalet, surveyed the area for an hour, and chose the campground for their night's sleep.

Sometime after twelve thirty on the morning of August 13, shrieks for help broke the natural silence around Granite Park Chalet. So unusual was any sound in the park at that time of night that it took the lodge's guests several tries before they could convince Tom and Nancy Walton that they heard screams somewhere below. Still believing that the commotion simply meant that a bear had wandered harmlessly into the camp and frightened some of the women, Walton led a party of thirteen people, including staff members and some brave guests, down the trail about five hundred yards to the campground.

No one expected the scene they encountered at the end of the trail. Roy Ducat, wrapped in camper Donald Gullett's sleeping bag, lay shivering and bleeding on the ground as several other campers sat on the roof of the cabin, their one flashlight beam weakened by their attempts to signal the chalet for help. Roy told a terrifying story of waking in the middle of the night when Julie whispered to him to play dead. Still numbed with sleep, he suddenly found himself flying sideways as a bear's massive paw knocked both teens a full five feet, and smelling the rancid odor of the animal's body, "as though a dozen dirty sheepdogs had come in from the rain," as Olsen retells it. In an astonishing act of self-control, Roy managed to remain silent as the bear's teeth penetrated his shoulder, then again when the teeth found his left arm and the backs of both of his legs. When the giant animal ripped into Julie's body, she screamed for help—and Roy realized that her screams were becoming more distant. The bear had dragged her and her sleeping bag off down the hill.

Miraculously, Roy leaped up and ran for the first sleeping camper he could find, awakening hiker Gullett, who saw the blood streaming from Roy's wounds and snapped into action. He wrapped the boy in his sleeping bag and woke campers Robert and Janet Klein, who took the escape route they had planned earlier in the evening and climbed on the roof of the nearby trail cabin. After several minutes of attempting to signal the chalet, they finally heard someone call down to them, "Is everything OK?"

"No!" Robert Klein responded, and followed this with, "Bear!"

The still-skeptical rescue party started down the trail moments later, including two doctors and young park ranger Joan Devereaux, who had led a hiking tour to the chalet that afternoon. Devereaux had the foresight to bring a shortwave radio. When the party arrived at the campsite and saw poor Roy Ducat covered in blood, they sprang into immediate action. Dr. Olgierd Lindan, a medical professor from Case Western Reserve University who had hiked to the chalet that day, administered first aid to Roy and prepared him to withstand a trip up the trail on a makeshift stretcher. Roy showed little concern for his own welfare, begging the rescuers to find Julie.

After much discussion, Walton and Devereaux determined that searching in pitch-blackness for the girl when they had only a few flashlights and a knife or two for self-defense could easily result in another mauling, and even loss of life. The party reluctantly turned toward the chalet and made their way uphill, Roy balanced between them on a pallet made from a bedspring found in the trail cabin.

At the chalet surgeon John Lipinski and his wife, Ann, who was a registered nurse, began doing what they could for Roy with limited supplies. Another guest came forward and introduced himself as a military physician, and stepped up to assist. Together with Dr. Lindan they treated Roy's wounds and his state of shock. Working tirelessly with the radio until she made contact with the emergency-trained rangers on duty at the scene of the forest fires, Devereaux obtained a promise that a helicopter would be on the way in a matter of minutes. Landing in the dark would be tough on any night in the northwestern wilderness, but that night smoke from the forest fires created a gray haze across the sky, and Devereaux knew the pilot would need more than a little help to find a safe place to put down the aircraft. She recruited many of the other campers to create a safe landing area for the helicopter that was now on its way.

Under Devereaux's direction the volunteers lit four fires around a clearing the helicopter had used once in the recent past and kept the fires burning as the helicopter approached. Several of the campers watched the bonfires closely for any sparks that could take flight and light a blaze in the surrounding forest, and their careful attention kept the fires from creating an even bigger problem at Granite Park Chalet.

"It was an eery sight and quite a haze was spread over the area because of the forest fires when I went in," the pilot, twenty-eight-year-old John Westover, told the Helena *Independent Record* much later the same day. This flight turned out to be only the first of three that Westover would make that night.

Volunteers unloaded the medical supplies Westover had brought and rushed them into the chalet's dining area, which had been pressed into service as an operating room. In minutes Westover took off in the helicopter with the now heavily bandaged Roy Ducat, taking him to a hospital in Kalispell.

Meanwhile, Fire Control Officer Gary Bunney, who had flown in on the helicopter, quickly organized a search party to find the missing Julie Helgeson somewhere in the forest. No one forgot for a moment that the grizzly bear was still at large, that this mission of mercy could be very dangerous . . . and that two hours had passed since Julie's disappearance.

Fueled by the knowledge that the girl was suffering and the fear that the bear might attack them at any moment, more than a dozen men made their way through the forest to the campground, and hiker Steve Pierre found a trail of blood leading into the woods. They followed this trail until they heard a tiny voice deep in the woods, calling faintly for help. Julie had managed to survive, though when the men saw her mangled body, they could hardly believe that she had withstood such a brutal attack. "It hurts," she told them in a whisper as the doctor in the party bent over her.

Dr. Lindan knew immediately what he was seeing. Puncture wounds in Julie's chest went through her lungs, and with each breath more oxygen escaped through them, making it nearly impossible for her to breathe at all. Her right forearm had been gnawed down to the bone, and wounds in her back and legs oozed blood. In the two hours since she had been attacked, Julie lay bleeding in this spot, and now the wounds no longer gushed. Dr. Lindan asked for coats and shirts from the men and covered her to keep her warm while others retrieved materials from the trail cabin to use as a stretcher.

The men brought Julie up the trail to the chalet, where surgeon Lipinski waited with the rest of the guests with medical training. They began their work as soon as Julie arrived, but it took no more than a moment or two before Dr. Lipinski recognized that Julie was already in the last moments of her life. He found no blood in her extremities, and her body worked so hard to breathe that it contorted with every gasp. He gave her an injection for pain and signaled the others to step back as Father Thomas Connolly, a priest who had hiked in with Steve Pierre the day before, held Julie's hand and administered last rites, even baptizing her as she let out her final breath. Julie died at 4:12 a.m.

No one in the chalet that night could know that, even as Julie lay dying, a second bear terrorized another campground some twenty miles across the park.

The Second Attack

At Trout Lake five young seasonal park employees and a puppy named Squirt planned on a quiet evening of fishing and camping on the night of August 12. Sixteen-year-old Paul Dunn, a busboy at East Glacier Lodge, was the only one of the party with no backcountry camping experience, but his companions all had camped in the woods many times: twenty-year-old Denise Huckle; brothers Ron and Ray Noseck, who were twenty-one and twenty-three; and Michele Koons, who was nineteen and working in the Lake McDonald Lodge gift shop that summer. They arrived at the logjam camp at the foot of the lake, set up their gear, hung up their food bag in a tree, and went to work fishing for their dinner while Michele kept an eye on the dog and finished assembling their camp.

Moments after Paul returned to the camp with his catch and began cooking, Michele spotted a bear through the smoke of the campfire. She alerted the others, and all five of them rushed up the hill, gathering up Squirt as they fled. From fifty yards away they watched the skinny grizzly so often reported at this campsite as it tore through their camp, eating their catch and everything else it could find. After nearly half an hour of this spectacle, the group decided to camp in their new position in the woods, where the bear might be a little less likely to look for scraps from humans' packs.

By this time darkness had fallen, so a full retreat back to Lake McDonald seemed as dangerous as staying put. Besides, everything the veteran campers knew about bears told them that if they didn't bother the bear, the bear wouldn't bother them. They agreed to stay where they were, and once the bear cleared out of the campsite, they retrieved their sleeping bags and whatever food they could. They built a fire at their new site and bedded down for the night.

Several hours later Denise awoke when she heard splashing sounds in the lake. She woke her friends, and they waited together as they saw the outline of the bear walk into the former camp and grab a sack of cookies they had left in hopes of distracting the animal from their current location. By this time it was four a.m., with dawn still as much as two hours off, so some of the group went back to sleep—but Denise remained vigilant and kept a tight hold on the puppy.

Not more than half an hour later, Denise saw the bear again, this time running straight for their current camp. She pulled her head into her sleeping bag and lay still, listening as the bear ripped through something that sounded like cloth. All of the campers kept still and silent while the bear rummaged through their camp, until Paul felt the animal bite into his sleeping bag and take hold of a piece of his sweatshirt.

Paul managed to slither out of his sleeping bag and run as the bear reared up on its hind legs. He climbed a tree to safety as Ron and Denise emerged as well, Ron tugging at Denise to get her to run even as she struggled with Squirt's collar. They ran for the shoreline and soon made it up into two trees while Paul shouted to Ray and Michele to run for their lives. Ray followed directions as quickly as he could, waylaid temporarily by the bear sniffing curiously at his own sleeping bag. He made a break for it when the bear turned to Michele's bag.

"He's ripping my arm!" the girl screamed as the bear bit into her sleeping bag. The bear had the zipper; she could not escape.

Seconds later she cried again, "Oh my God, I'm dead!"

The bear took hold of Michele's sleeping bag and dragged the girl and the bag out of the campsite and into the dark.

When they were sure that there was nothing they could do for Michele, the four campers grabbed their shoes and made the four-mile trek over Howe Ridge to the nearest road, where a couple just beginning a hike quickly offered to take them to the nearest ranger station in their car.

When he arrived in the station at eight ten a.m. on the morning of August 13, Ranger Leonard Landa had already heard about the bear mauling that had resulted in the death of Julie Helgeson just a few hours earlier, so it seemed impossible that the four campers standing before him could be telling him of another bear attack on the same night. He sent Ray and Denise home and led Paul and Ron on a trek back to Trout Lake, and together they discovered exactly what the campers had described: the main campsite in shambles, and no sign of Michele Koons. They continued up the hill in the direction that Paul had seen the bear drag the girl, and eventually they made what was likely the most gruesome discovery of Landa's career: the remains of Michele's body, much of it gnawed away by the attacking grizzly.

A short time later pilot John Westover made his third mercy flight in less than twelve hours, this time to transport the body of Michele Koons from the park.

By the end of the day Monday, rangers with "high-powered rifles" had killed two grizzlies near the Granite Park Chalet and another one in the Trout Lake area. A fourth bear met its death from rangers' rifles as well. Examination and testing at a later date revealed that the Trout Lake bear was the one that attacked and killed Michele Koons. The examinations of the bears killed in the Granite Park area were inconclusive.

THE AFTERMATH

Why had two grizzlies in two different places suddenly attacked human campers, when such a thing had never happened in the park's fifty-seven-year history?

Speculation ran rampant. Some suggested that the number and frequency of the lightning strikes the night before the attacks could have agitated the bears. "There seems to be an association between the lightning and the attacks," park superintendent Keith Nielson told the Associated Press in an article published on Monday, August 14, 1967. He noted that a park service biologist was en route to the park to try to determine what had caused this marked change in the bears' behavior.

In the interim a bevy of experts stepped up to offer their opinions. Dr. Frank Craighead Jr., a researcher who worked in collaboration with his brother, John Craighead, on extensive studies of the grizzly bear (and who would later write the book *Track of the Grizzly),* said that these confrontations were to be expected given the increase of the park's popularity in recent years. In the Kalispell newspaper the *Daily Inter Lake,* Craighead suggested "that because of the increase of visitor use of such areas the incidence of contact between grizzly and man has been expected to increase."

Faye Couey of the Montana Fish and Game Department rejected the idea that lightning had driven the bears to violence—as well as comments by others that a sparse huckleberry crop and dry weather may have caused the animals to attack. "Couey, who probably knows grizzly bears as well as anybody in the area, said he doesn't feel anyone knows grizzly bear psychology well enough to explain the death of the two girls." In the same article in the *Daily Inter Lake,* Covey continued, "I have never heard any theories based upon actual studies which would indicate the bears are incited to violence by lightning or by the extended periods of hot, dry weather. I would be very much against the complete elimination of grizzly bears in this area, because of these two incidents. We respect the grizzly bear."

Grizzlies tore up many camps in the area, Couey went on, so it was only a matter of time before something like this happened. "Camp bears are used to garbage and camp food and they never get enough," he told the *Daily Inter Lake*. "People who sleep out in an area where these bears are take a big chance. The chance is not merely getting camp equipment torn up or being run off by a bear, they are taking their lives in their hands, as the recent incidents prove."

It took less than a week (lightning speed in 1967) before the general public began to comment on the matter. An open letter to the National Park Service, published in the *Daily Inter Lake* on Friday, August 18, 1967, called for the government agency to allow citizens to "have the protection of a sealed firearm of sufficient caliber" to take out a grizzly if the situation arose. Editorials in the *Independent Record* and the *Daily Inter Lake* begged for patience and caution in response to apparent public outcry for extermination of the grizzly bears. "Persons hiking and camping in the wilderness must be made aware that they have invaded the domain of wild animals and advised of the precautions they must take," said an editorial on August 18. "It would be a shame to eliminate the park's grizzlies because of last weekend's tragedies." Another piece in the Sunday, August 20, *Daily Inter Lake* noted, "When there is a flood anywhere, most people immediately want to build a dam, and it has been proven this is not always the answer . . . Time and study are needed before reaching a decision that could affect the welfare of all Northwest Montana and its people."

When the park service finally issued a report nearly a year later, it stated that a whole host of theories had been explored, and no specific conclusion could explain why two bears in two different parts of the park attacked campers within hours of each other. The park made a number of definitive moves to prevent more attacks, but one stands out from the rest: It closed the dumps at Granite Park and in the northwestern arm of the park at Polebridge, and rangers began to enforce the park's long-standing but largely ignored rules against feeding bears.

SHATTERED PEACE

No further deaths from bear attacks took place for nine years after the events of August 13, 1967, but the next events bore more than a passing similarity to the killings of Julie Helgeson and Michele Koons.

Twenty-two-year-old Mary Pat Mahoney, camping with a group of friends at Many Glacier Campground on September 23, 1976, took every precaution the park service recommended to avoid any confrontation with a bear. Her group set up camp in a regulation campsite, stored their food in bear-proof containers out of reach of any marauding bears, slept in tents rather than out in the open, left their cosmetics at home, and even planned their trip for a day when none of the girls were menstruating. They left their unlocked car no more than ten feet from their tent, in case they had to dash for cover. Nonetheless, at about seven a.m., a young grizzly bear dragged Mary Pat from her tent, mauled her to death, and proceeded to eat her. Her companions managed to escape and run for help, and within an hour and a half, two grizzly bears were dead—shot by park rangers. One of the bears had human blood between its front claws.

This time the park service had known which bears to locate and destroy, because the animals had a brief but vivid history of visiting campsites and chasing people. The two adolescent bears showed up just a week before at an illegal camp at Iceberg Lake, not far from Many Glacier Campground. The campers had not stored their food in bear-proof containers or taken the precaution of hanging it up out of bears' reach, so the bears helped themselves to what they found. Two days later the bears ran into two hikers near Ptarmigan Lake, who discarded their packs and ran off—leaving the bears to eat heartily and further reinforcing the connection between people and food.

A couple of days later, the same bears showed up at Many Glacier Campground and ate from a garbage can, and over the next several days, they began to approach humans directly: first a sunbather, then two fishermen, and then campers in an area that had been closed to camping because of the behavior of these two bears. By the time Mary Pat Mahoney and her friends camped at Many Glacier, the pattern was established. Any camper would have been in danger from these two habituated creatures.

On July 23, 1980, Jane Ammerman and her boyfriend, Kim Eberly, two nineteen-year-olds on their day off from working at Lake McDonald Lodge, decided to spend the night at the St. Mary resort area. Despite instructions posted all over the developed campground—an area created more for trailers and mobile homes than for tent camping—the pair chose what the *Chicago Tribune* later described as "a spit of land between two lakes on the eastern edge of the park" and set up camp outside of the developed area in the thicket alongside a pleasant stream. The *Tribune* continues, "They apparently presumed all the park's grizzly bears were spending the summer in the distant high country, as is common."

No one saw what happened next, but at noon the next day, a fisherman came upon the mauled body of one of the teenagers, and a search by park rangers soon turned up the second one. "Both had been partly consumed," wrote Stephen Herrero in his book *Bear Attacks: Their Causes and Avoidance*. Park superintendent Philip Iverson recruited Herrero to serve on a board of inquiry to explore the two young people's deaths.

The inquiry revealed a dangerous situation. "About half a mile from their camp was a small garbage dump," Herrero wrote. "The dump was on land that was a private inholding surrounded by the Blackfoot Indians . . . Park officials had tried to get this dump closed, but the area was outside their jurisdiction." Herrero surmised that the grizzly that attacked Jane and Kim probably was on its way to or from the dump early on the morning of July 24 when it came upon the teenagers sleeping on top of their tent during the warm, humid night.

Indeed, St. Mary area residents had seen just such a bear, a three-year-old grizzly that foraged in the dump much too often for their comfort. Some residents of the Blackfoot tribe had tried to shoot the bear before this, knowing that its acclimation to humans could be dangerous. With two teens now dead, the Blackfoot Indians had reason to pursue the bear aggressively, and they found and killed it in the vicinity of the grisly deaths that same day. An autopsy revealed remains of the two teens in the bear's digestive tract.

While the deaths left the 1980 seasonal park staff shaken, this incident did not cause the kind of panic and dread that the 1967 deaths triggered. Park management put the pieces together fairly quickly, tracing the causes of the attack to violations—albeit out of the park's control—of the established protocols for preventing bears from becoming habituated to human contact.

In September 1980, thirty-three-year-old Laurence Gordon left on a solo camping trip through the Belly River valley, choosing to spend the night at Elizabeth Lake. The warnings against hiking and camping alone go well beyond Glacier National Park to include any park, in any state or country, anywhere in the world, and the Glacier park rangers admonished him for taking on the Montana wilderness unaided . . . but Gordon clearly felt confident about his outdoor skills.

It's hard to say exactly when the grizzly bear came into his camp and attacked him, but what remained of Gordon was discovered on October 3. The inquiry into his death resulted in some certainty that he died of a bear attack, although it left the door open to the idea that Gordon could have died of another cause and simply been scavenged by a bear accustomed to finding food in one form or another at the campsite.

Seven years would pass before the next death by grizzly, but the cause of this one clearly lay in the relative inexperience of the hiker involved. Budding forty-year-old wildlife photographer Charles Gibbs, hiking with his wife, Glenda, came upon a female grizzly and her three cubs on the slope of Elk Mountain. Charles eagerly set out to get closer to the bears for a great photo, while Glenda continued on the trail to the couple's car. With no one to tell Charles when he was getting too close, his family had to piece together the end of the story from the photos on the last roll of film he would ever shoot. Charles tried to follow the bears, even when they moved purposefully away from him, and he apparently got some great shots of the sow turning toward him to challenge him. When he still didn't move away, the sow charged him. "His last photograph showed the bear at about 50 yards and moving toward him," an article in *Backpacker* magazine revealed.

On July 27, 1987, twenty-nine-year-old Gary Goeden, a night auditor during the summer months at the park, took an off-trail solo hike that led to Natahki Lake in the Many Glacier area. The last anyone knew about Gary's whereabouts on that July day was that he loved to hike Glacier's trails, that he had headed out alone, and that he chose to strike out into the backcountry rather than follow an established route. No trace of him came to light until September 1, when his partially consumed remains were discovered near the lake. We will never know for certain whether Gary encountered a bear on the trail and could not escape or whether he died of some other cause and became a meal of opportunity for a passing grizzly. Gary's name became one more note on the list of people who hiked alone and never returned, further warning to people who risk their lives on wilderness trails in the name of solitude and self-discovery.

Tolerance or Extinction?

When experienced backcountry hiker John Petranyi met a mother grizzly bear and her two cubs on the Loop Trail, in the Upper McDonald Valley half a mile below Granite Park Chalet, park management and wildlife officials throughout the region raised questions about what to do next.

Petranyi, a forty-year-old visitor from Madison, Wisconsin, was hiking alone in the middle of the day on October 3, 1992, when he encountered the three grizzlies. The sow attacked him and mauled him to death, and she and her two cubs fed on his body before leaving the area. Eight days later all three bears were dead, exterminated by park staff.

A report published in the *Christian Science Monitor* examined what it called "one of the worst grizzly bear attacks ever," an event caused by "the increasing number of human-bear encounters as grizzly-bear habitat continues to shrink in the lower 48 states."

With declining amounts of habitat in the vicinity around the park as northwestern Montana became a popular location for new homes and larger communities, grizzlies and people were coming face to face more often than ever before. Glacier National Park's popularity grew as well—in 1992, the park hosted 2.2 million visitors, up from 1.6 million annually in the 1980s. More contact between humans and bears had become inevitable.

"And we've noticed a new trend," park chief ranger Steve Frye told the *Monitor.* "People are seeking more solitary areas off the beaten path in the park than they used to. Grizzlies can't live on an island, so we must maintain habitat outside the park system where they can move freely. Bears just don't understand administrative boundaries."

Experts from all aspects of the grizzly habitat conundrum weighed in on the issue. Mike Bader, executive director of the

Alliance for the Wild Rockies, called for closure of "large seg-ments of bear habitat on a seasonal basis . . . When managers know it's a poor food year, they need to be more flexible and make unpopular decisions to close areas for the bears."

Charles Jonkel, director of the Border Grizzly Project, disagreed with the decision to destroy the culprit bears. "There was no historical biological evidence to support their premise that the bears would link killing the victim with feeding on him," he said. "Grizzlies do not have a predator-prey relationship with man."

Chris Servheen, grizzly bear recovery coordinator for the US Fish and Wildlife Service, stayed firm in the opinion he had expressed to the park service when the bear hunt began. "We don't tolerate those types of aggressive bears," he told the *Monitor*. "It's dangerous and it's teaching its cubs things and that's not the type of animal that we tolerate in griz-zly habitat." He said that cubs learn everything from their mother, so this attack made them "a lost cause."

When another family unit of three bears—a mother and two cubs—stalked, killed, and devoured twenty-six-year-old Craig Dahl while he hiked a winding trail above Two Medicine Valley on May 17, 1998, forensic science had so improved that searchers knew without a doubt which bears had done it. What had turned this particular sow to see peo-ple as food, however, remained a mystery even as scientists examined hair and scat at the scene for DNA matches with the tagged bears throughout the park. They determined that the mother bear, known as Chocolate Legs, had chased Dahl downhill for several hundred yards before killing him—direct evidence of intentional predatory behavior.

Glacier's chief wildlife biologist, Steve Gniadek, knew Chocolate Legs well. By the time the bear was just eighteen months old, she had already become habituated to people, foraging through trash barrels at people's homes and allowing tourists to photograph her in "bear jams" of cars along the park's roads. Park personnel captured this bear back in 1983 and moved her out of the area, and she lived a normal bear's life until just a few months before she led the attack on Craig Dahl—when she and her cubs came to Two Medicine Campground as if there were no people there. By September 1997 the three bears had begun charging at hikers.

"Current bear-management policy in Glacier Park, Montana, dictates that such bears be killed or captured and removed from the park after one aggressive incident," wrote Herrero in an update to his 1985 book. "Such action is probably necessary to give an acceptable level of safety. But this new toughness toward grizzly bears must come in conjunction with a similar toughness toward ignorant and careless park visitors, whose food or garbage starts a grizzly off on such a path."

CHAPTER 7

Rushing Rocks and Snow: Death by Avalanche

No one saw it coming.

Glacier National Park superintendent Jack Emmert would tell the media that the mountainside "broke suddenly without warning" on May 26, 1953, despite the presence of watchmen stationed to keep an eye on the ninety-foot-high snowdrifts on the mountainsides lining Going-to-the-Sun Road.

This particular snowfield, however, did not show any of the telltale signs of falling. The watchmen did not see cracks shooting through the snowpack or hear the "whumpfing" sound that means that a weak layer under the surface has begun to collapse. What they did see were four men working on an avalanche that had dumped many feet of snow on the road before they arrived: mixed gang foreman George Beaton, seasonal employee William Whitford, general equipment operator Frederick Klein, and park employee Eugene Sullivan.

"We were working one mile above the Garden Wall road camp," Sullivan told the *Daily Inter Lake* the following day, on May 27, 1953. "We were working on a slide that had come down during the night."

That slide skittered down the Garden Wall on Monday, May 25, a little more than half a mile from the Garden Wall work camp.

"Fred had just brought me a 50-pound box of dynamite and I had the detonator," said Sullivan, "and I was just going to start punching some holes in the snow so we could blast out some of the snow to let the Snow-go plow go through."

These four crew members had decades of experience in removing these high volumes of snow. They had succeeded in the job year after year without any serious mishaps. They had plenty of snow removal equipment, including a large Sno-go three-auger, two-unit rotary tractor plow for removing big drifts and frozen snow walls. They were one of several crews working their way toward Logan Pass, and their position seemed secure enough that road crew foreman Ray Price left the crew and went up the road at about ten a.m. to check on the general road clearing operations in progress.

"It had been raining Sunday and Monday and there were 10 inches of fresh snow when we went to work," Sullivan said. "I asked the boys, 'How does she look, boys?' They said, 'Hell, she won't come down.'"

Hardly a moment later the snow began to move.

"We heard it all right," said Sullivan. "It was wet snow and it slid without making much noise. When I saw it coming, I jumped down in a hole about 5 or 6 feet deep, which the Snow-go had cut."

Sullivan found himself at a secure but terrifying vantage point. "Bill Whitford was in the Snow-go," he said. "From where I was crouched in the hole, I saw the snow hit the Snow-go and I saw it start to go over the side of the mountain. Blackie [Beaton] and Freddy were running down the road. I stayed in the hole and wet snow covered me."

In seconds Gene Sullivan was buried alive. The wave of moving snow swept Beaton and Klein over the edge of the road as well and dashed the Sno-go plow to pieces on the rocks below. "Parts of it were scattered down the 60 degree slope for more than three-quarters of a mile," the *Daily Inter Lake* reported the following day.

The time was about ten forty-five a.m.

When Price returned to the area where the crew had been clearing the original snow slide at about eleven thirty a.m., he saw in an instant that another slide had covered the first—and that none of his men or equipment were in sight. Hoping against hope, he made his way down the road to the next-closest road crew to see if Beaton's crew had retreated there in advance of the second slide. No one had seen the missing men. They all came to the same conclusion: The men were buried under the avalanche.

Price and the lower road crew headed back up the road as quickly as they could and began digging by hand to find the missing men. It didn't take long to find Fred Klein, who was near the surface and unconscious, but still breathing as the men cleared snow from his face and body. They soon discovered Bill Whitford as well, thrown from the Snow-go and no longer breathing. Whitford had died instantly from a broken neck, sustained as he rolled down the slope some thirteen hundred feet.

By twelve thirty p.m. Price and his men got a message

radioed back to park headquarters, notifying them of the accident and requesting emergency assistance. While Jack Emmert directed the overall rescue operation by radio from park headquarters, Assistant Superintendent George W. Miller and park engineer Richard Montgomery handled on-the-scene coordination. Crews arrived and began to shovel by hand to clear the road, while a front-end loader shovel removed the layers of ice that remained. Still there was no sign of Beaton or Sullivan.

As more and more people arrived to help, digging progressed as quickly as it could. At about seven p.m. the crews found Sullivan, unconscious but breathing, five feet deep in the snow. "Just as the snow started to cover me up, I raised up a little to keep it loose around my body," he told the *Daily Inter Lake* the next day. "Then it covered me up and packed me in tight. I had a couple of inches leeway around my head and I worked a little space loose around my hands. I was conscious quite a while after I was buried."

Crew members rushed Sullivan to the Garden Wall road camp, where a doctor from Columbia Falls was waiting to assist and revive any remaining survivors. He administered first aid and oxygen, and within the hour Sullivan had regained consciousness—and he immediately told the rescue crews where he had last seen Beaton. In minutes Sullivan was in an ambulance on his way to Sisters of Mercy Hospital, while rescuers, buoyed by their success in locating Sullivan, doubled down on their efforts to find Beaton.

Now the operation would continue after dark, with the possibility of finding George Beaton alive. The park brought in power equipment and lights, and construction company

General-Shea-Morrison in Hungry Horse sent up additional equipment to help. Men from Great Northern relieved exhausted rescue crew members at midnight and at four a.m. as the digging progressed throughout the night.

At 3:17 a.m. a bloodhound named Joy and her owner, George Talbot of Corvallis, arrived to assist in finding the last missing crewman. Using one of Beaton's slippers retrieved from his cabin, Talbot gave Joy the scent and they picked their way with care down the slope. It took Joy about two hours to find Beaton, but, as the crew expected by that time, he had not survived the fall.

Later in the day on May 28, the park awarded Joy a medal, making her an official park ranger.

"The tragedy marked the first fatalities ever suffered in the history of Going-to-the-Sun highway clearing operations, first opened in 1933," the *Daily Inter Lake* concluded, completing its coverage of the events of May 27 and 28, 1953.

Emmert later emphasized that the park takes every precaution to ensure that the general public is not placed in the path of a potential avalanche on Going-to-the-Sun Road. "The park has no record of any persons being injured by avalanches while the highway has been open to tourists," he told the media. "We sent Richard T. Montgomery, park engineer, to the avalanche school for skiers at Alta, Utah, last winter to study avalanche conditions. Every precaution to protect the visitor and employee is taken here at the park."

The Warning Signs

Geological and meteorological science has progressed since 1953, so now we have a better idea of the indicators of an

avalanche. Should you ever find yourself in an area of ⌣
cier National Park where long slopes and large snowfields
create an environment for suddenly sliding snowpack, watch
for these telltale signs of impending danger, according to the
American Avalanche Association:

Recent avalanches. If there's been an avalanche in the
last day or so, the potential for another one is very high.

Signs of unstable snow as you travel. Watch for crack-
ing or collapsing snowpack, and listen for hollow, drum-like
sounds on hard snow. Snowfields that are about to erupt in
an avalanche often (but not always) make a "whumpfing"
sound.

Heavy snowfall or rain in the last twenty-four hours
can create an unstable situation.

Windblown snow can create "wind slabs," big sheets of
snow that can suddenly crumble.

Significant warming or increasing temperatures.
Warmth, when combined with gravity, can encourage snow
to creep—and eventually race—downhill.

Persistent weak layers. Weakened layers of snow beneath
you can cause a sudden avalanche as you pass through. You
may have no idea that these layers exist, so check with visitor
centers and/or rangers in the park to find out where there are
avalanche advisories before you set out on a snow-covered
trail or mountain.

It may be tough to perceive these warning signs if you
are speeding down a slope on skis or a snowboard, as thirty-
seven-year-old Brian C. Wright of Whitefish discovered in
March 2010. Wright planned to spend several days on a solo
ski and snowboard trip in the park, and he kept in touch with

friends by texting them periodically with his location. On Tuesday, March 30, at six p.m., his text told friends that he was on Mount Shields. They followed up with him the next day, but Wright stopped responding to their messages, a sign that something had gone wrong.

One of the friends located Wright's vehicle at the Fielding Ranger Station trailhead, so he skied the trail up to Mount Shields—and he spotted Wright's body, "high in a gully within the slide path of a recent avalanche," according to a park news release on April 2, 2010. "Rangers believe Wright triggered a large slab avalanche while snowboarding on Mt. Shields at approximately 1 p.m. Wednesday, March 31." Only a short while before, Wright had called his mother on his mobile phone from the summit of the mountain.

Evidence-gathering activities in the area discovered that Wright had made two trips up to the face of Mount Shields, one in an open area with little forestation and another on the northeast face. Rangers concluded that the second route—on Peak 6996, also known as Palindrome Peak or Little Shields—triggered the avalanche, sending snowpack skittering two thousand feet down the mountain. "Wright's body was about 200–300 yards above the end (toe) of the avalanche slide path," the release continued. "Investigating rangers believe he tumbled approximately 2,000 feet before his body came to rest at an elevation of 5,427 feet."

A full investigation of the incident by a team of experts concluded that a three-day winter storm that had blown through the area just before Wright's trip to Mount Shields left the underlying snowpack "layered and highly variable," according to a report in the *Missoulian*. Investigators noted in their report, "Upon summiting, we experienced collapsing ('whumpfing') of the snowpack." This meant that one to two feet of new snow from the storm sat on a layer of "unstable crystals."

Tracks indicated that Wright had intersected the avalanche run, and 533 feet below the point where he ran into it, the investigators found bloodstained snow. "A snowboard track led out of the avalanche path at that point, descending the mountain to 5,868 feet, where Wright's snowboard was found," the *Missoulian* continued. Wright's body was found 441 feet farther down the mountain.

"Officials will never know for sure what happened because Wright was alone," the Associated Press noted when the report on the cause of death was released on April 20.

THE NEW YEAR'S CLIMB

On December 27, 1969, five young men from towns and cities across Montana came together to climb Mount Cleveland, the highest peak in the park at 10,448 feet, over the course of four days. Their plan, despite warnings to the contrary by park rangers, was to take on the peak's north slope, the most difficult side to scale when the mountain is covered with snow and ice.

"Apparently a couple of them have already climbed the northwest slope we recommend to climbers," said Ruben Hart, chief ranger for the park in 1969 and 1970, in an interview with the *Daily Inter Lake* on January 4, 1970. "It's not a genuine climb but what climbers call a mountaineer scramble."

That didn't interest these five adventurers, however. They wanted to achieve a mountain climbing first, scaling the sheer, vertical north face of the mountain in winter. They wanted to do this even though only one member of their party had any significant climbing experience.

So the five youths stuck to their plan and took a boat out of Waterton, Alberta, ten miles to the south end of Waterton Lake on the last Saturday in December. Bigfork resident James Anderson, who was eighteen; eighteen-year-old Jerry Kanzler of Bozeman; Mark Levitan from Helena, who was twenty; and Clare Pogreba and Ray Martin, both twenty-two years old and both from Butte, started their trek to make base camp and begin their climb the following day.

Four days later, when none of the young men contacted their families to let them know they had returned from the mountain, the families began an informal search for them. At that point they believed that the boys were simply taking the return route slowly, basing their return on the "give or take a day" schedule they had provided to their families. When James Anderson's brother Bud went to the base of the mountain on Thursday, January 1, to see if the climbing party was ready for pickup, however, he saw no sign of them. He made the trip again on Friday and discovered that they had not been back to their camp at all.

This time he contacted authorities, and Waterton warden Jack Christenson joined Anderson to search for the boys. Together they found a cache of skis and equipment on the edge of the timber coming out of Cleveland Creek, a sign that they were moving in the right direction—but that the climbers had not come back from the mountain to their base camp. Christenson called in search and rescue personnel, and two fixed-wing aircraft made an aerial reconnaissance trip. "The two pilots reported seeing tracks which could have been man or animal," wrote reporter Jim Peterson in the *Daily Inter Lake*. "They also reported a small snowslide on the northwest slope. Latest information seems to indicate the lost climbers are not in the area of the slide."

Friday's search continued into Saturday, made more complicated by low clouds at about six thousand feet, which made efforts to search from the air by a helicopter from Malmstrom Air Force Base virtually impossible. Blowing snow at ground level hampered rescue crews as well, though one three-man search party made an important discovery: The five young men had split into two groups, a two-member party and a three-member party. The tracks from the two-member party led nearly vertically toward the north slope, while the other three men had headed to the northwest. It looked likely that the second party intended to circle the peak and come in above the north slope climbers, perhaps to help them with their ascent.

The split happened just above the second base camp, where the climbers had left their tents and food before beginning the arduous climb up the rocky terrain. "All we know now is they're lost somewhere in the rocks above the camp we discovered today," said Hart to reporters. "That covers several square miles. The problem is compounded by the fact the rocky terrain is shaded by the mountain and hence quite black. It's difficult to spot anything."

On Sunday, January 4, three professional climbers from Banff National Park in Alberta, Canada, joined the search to explore the north slope and look for clues of the young climbers' route. Discussion of next steps took the weather into consideration as well. Hart told the *Daily Inter Lake* that he didn't expect temperatures to drop much below zero, but "that can be mighty cold when you can't move around—and moving around is a problem on a steep rock face."

By now there were twenty-six men searching the mountain, ten of them professional climbers, and park superintendent William Briggle told the paper that Monday would be "make or break day" for the search. He noted that he would soon have to make the extraordinarily difficult decision whether to expand the operation or call it off. "We'll continue searching as long as we dare," he said, "but at the same time, we must consider the safety of our rescue teams."

Climbers from Jasper National Park in Alberta and Grand Teton National Park in Wyoming arrived to aid in the search of the north face. When Waterton Lake froze in subzero temperatures and the boat could no longer get through with supplies, the park rented a helicopter from Johnson Flying Service in Missoula to airlift supplies to the search crews, while another helicopter continued the aerial search. Meanwhile, hikers carried supplies up the mountain to the professional climbers, braving an eight-hour round-trip with full packs in temperatures plunging to minus thirty degrees Fahrenheit.

The professionals discovered snow caves on the north slope, as well as some tracks made by three climbers, indicating that at least some of the party made it that far. They refocused their efforts on the part of the mountain above the timberline, well above 6,000 feet. From here the sheer north face rises almost straight up for 4,000 feet. "Our climbers are inspecting every ledge, crack and crevice for signs," said Dan

Nelson, coordinator of the alpine search. "So far, no sight and no sound."

The search began to draw curiosity seekers as well, including a number of private pilots who began circling the mountain in their small planes. The flyers did much more harm than good, causing small snow slides on the mountain as they passed. Briggle asked for and received the Federal Aviation Agency's cooperation in ordering all private aircraft out of the area.

For a total of nine days, the search for the five young adventurers continued. Finally, on January 9, Superintendent Briggle and Waterton Lakes National Park superintendent Tom Ross agreed that the fifty-mile-an-hour winds, heavy snowfall, and the clear possibility of avalanches made further searching too dangerous for the rescuers. They consulted with the families and issued a joint statement, bringing the search to an end for the winter. "The statement snapped the last thin thread of remaining hope, and the secret of the fate of the five youths will have to be unlocked next summer," Jim Peterson wrote on January 9. The twenty climbers and base camp support party who remained at the mountain began the twelve-mile trek, using skis and snowshoes, to meet snowmobiles that took them to Waterton.

The search had revealed some important information, even if it did not find the five missing men. Ranger Doug Erskine made it to the top of Mount Cleveland and checked the register there, and found no indication that the five climbers had been there.

"The recovery now will have to await the spring conditions and personnel will take up toward the end of June or early July where they have left off now," Briggle said. "But it will have to wait until it is again safe to send men and equipment to the high mountain levels to complete the operation."

So the park staff and rescue personnel, the families, and the community waited. There was no question that the five young men had perished on the mountain, but the manner and circumstances of their deaths remained a mystery. The wait grew longer as late spring snows created more dangers, with deep accumulations of two feet and more. As June arrived, the search resumed, with teams heading up the mountain every other day, following what clues they could find to narrow the field and discover the bodies. They found an ice ax, a hat, and a climber's pack and knew that they were getting closer.

Finally, on June 29, 1970, the park announced that the first body of a young climber had been found. It was high up the peak at just about 7,500 feet, spotted in an ice column—and rescuers chopped through fourteen feet of ice to retrieve it. The body turned out to be Ray Martin, still in the rope harness he was wearing when he died—and searchers were certain that the rope, extending upward, would lead to at least one more body, and probably more.

The body of the second boy, James Anderson, came to light on July 1 just thirty feet from Ray Martin. Anderson's body was buried deeper, however, and the recovery team had to tunnel through eighteen feet of snow and debris to reach it and free it from the mountain's icy grip. For the first time a cause of death could be proposed: The boys were buried in an avalanche. "The thinking of recovery personnel is the youths were overwhelmed at higher level on the mountain by an avalanche and swept down into a small basin and held there in the debris," wrote Larry Stem of the *Daily Inter Lake*. "Additional accumulation of winter snow turning into ice locked them in place in the basin where the recovery operation is being continued today."

Now, as the weather cleared, rescuers could bring in a pump and hose and melt down the ice and snow covering the remaining bodies, shortening the work of recovering them. On July 3 they brought down the bodies of Jerry Kanzler, Mark Levitan, and Clare Pogreba.

The eight men on the final retrieval team included Larry Feser, Jerry DeSanto, Fred Goodsell, Paul Roney, Ronald Hurd, William Hutchinson, Donald Juneau, and Larry Sonstelie, who spent five weeks working their way up and down the mountain until all five boys were found and their remains returned to their families.

As writer Larry Stem noted, the best summation of this tragedy came from Kurt Seel, mountain climber and a naturalist at Waterton Lakes National Park. "That mountain doesn't give a damn about anyone," Seel told Stem. "It's not unconquerable. It is treacherous. In the summertime rocks roll constantly. In the winter time it's the wind and the snow. That mountain is alive all the time."

Part of its life, apparently, involves taking the lives of others.

CHAPTER 8

Without Warning:
Falling Objects

WE CAN CARRY BEAR SPRAY, ALWAYS HIKE IN PAIRS OR groups, stay off of mountains in the dead of winter, drive the speed limit, watch our step around streams and waterfalls, stay behind barriers, carry survival gear, and obey every other rule Glacier National Park recommends for its visitors . . . and nature may still find a way to bring a life to a sudden, unexpected end in the blink of an eye.

A handful of people—just eight, as of this writing—have managed to be in exactly the wrong place at the right time, just as a massive boulder or a tree started to move of its own volition. While deaths under falling objects are an exception rather than the rule, they bring a heightened level of awareness of the towering mountains above the road, the stability of trees in the face of extreme weather conditions, and the speed with which a chunk of ice may slide down a hill and bring someone's life to an abrupt, unceremonious close.

Men at Work

The first two people who lost their lives this way did so on Going-to-the-Sun Road, but not in the way you might think. Carl Rosenquist and Gust Swanson were construction workers in the early 1930s on the massive, $2.5 million project, laboring to remove millions of cubic yards of rock to create a foundation on which the road could wind along the edges of mountainsides for fifty-two miles.

The workers moved very slowly through the wilderness area, setting off series of small explosions to remove areas of rock while doing the least possible damage to the walls rising above them. Tunnels provided some of the greatest challenges, as workers could only bore through rock at the rate of about sixty-four inches in twenty-four hours—an extraordinarily slow pace, considering that the East Side Tunnel alone is 408 feet long.

Even these small, controlled blasts disrupted the stability of some mountainsides, however, as Rosenquist discovered on August 26, 1931. The exact circumstances of his death have not been recorded for posterity, but we know that the culprit was a falling rock.

In Swanson's case the mountains sent a more vehement response to the blasting. On July 14, 1932, a rockslide—most likely triggered by one of the small explosions—careened down the mountainside about a mile and a half east of Logan Pass, burying the worker and taking his life.

(One more death took place during the construction of Going-to-the-Sun Road, though in this case the falling object turned out to be the worker himself. In 1926, Charles Rudbergin lowered himself down from a cliff on a rope to perform some duty crucial to the project, but the rope slipped and he plummeted to the roadbed below.)

This same kind of random chance took the life of another worker in the park years later. Andrew Jackson Aldrich, a cook's helper in a Civilian Conservation Corps camp near Kalispell, went out to walk across the camp to deliver a message on January 6, 1939. Winter days in Glacier bring all kinds of hazards—bone-stiffening cold, whiteout snowstorms, blinding sun flashing off of icy surfaces—but in this case the force of the wind posed the greatest threat to this twenty-year-old man. At exactly the moment he passed under a tree, a branch fell and smashed him in the head. The park records that the branch had been left in place after being chopped through, but whether this was a natural event or one caused by another worker's negligence, the result was the same. "He was the third in the Andrew Jackson Aldrich line to die by an accident," a notation at OurFamilyTree.org tells us, "and the Aldrich family would no longer name a son Andrew Jackson."

Another vindictive tree took the life of thirty-three-year-old Keith Moors on December 28, 1967, while he worked as a "cat-skinner," the term loggers use for a bulldozer operator, for the Canyon Logging Company in Columbia Falls. Moors was working inside Glacier National Park in the Nyack area when he got off his crawler tractor to adjust a choker cable. He chose to do this on the downhill side of a large tree that his coworkers had just sawed partway through. The loggers above Moors called to him to get out of the way, but the tractor engine drowned out their cries, and he didn't move. There was nothing to be done—gravity had already taken over the operation. The tree fell, killing Moors instantly.

Visits Foreshortened

Since Glacier became a unit of the National Park Service in 1910, only four visitors have had the extraordinarily bad luck of finding themselves under a falling object. Of these, the most gut-wrenching story involves tiny Bernida Marie Byrd, who was just eight months old when the accident occurred in August 1951. She and her parents, Mr. and Mrs. Duane Byrd of Martin City, were out for a pleasant ride through the park on a Sunday afternoon when a tree fell on their car. Both parents survived, but the baby's injuries were too severe, and her life ended abruptly that day.

In 1962, on the same June day that saw Elberta Dickman drown in McDonald Creek (see chapter 1), Alice Jean Leckie, visiting from Winnipeg, Manitoba, rode alone in the back-seat of the car driven by her husband, Gordon, as they toured Going-to-the-Sun Road. The Leckies' daughter, Maureen, also rode in the front seat. As the car passed the Garden Wall heading east, about a mile and a half after Logan Pass, a massive boulder—weighing some four hundred pounds and about two and a half feet around—suddenly sprang from the wall and fell toward the Leckies' car. Gathering momentum as it fell, it crashed through the left rear window of the car and flattened Alice in the backseat. She was killed in an instant. Gordon, shaken and stricken with grief, was transported to a hospital in Alberta and treated for shock, along with his daughter, who was physically unharmed.

Thirty-four years would pass before another fatality by falling object took place on Going-to-the-Sun Road. This time, in 1996, the tourist had come all the way from Japan to enjoy the park. Tsuyoshi Kamochi, who was thirty, and his sister, Yoko Kamochi, lived in the Washington, D.C., area while they attended school there, and they made the trip across the country to explore the natural sights. They were driving along the road on a pleasant June day, admiring the many viewpoints and expansive landscapes, when the mountainside close beside them suddenly erupted into a rockslide. Seeing the wall of boulders coming at them, Tsuyoshi slammed the car into reverse and hit the gas, making a bold escape that very nearly worked . . . until the hillside released another wave of rocks and soil and buried the front of the vehicle. Authorities later said that the slide covered up to one hundred fifty feet of the winding road. "Survival was defined by a matter of feet," wrote Vince Moravek in his book *It Happened in Glacier National Park.* "The front half of the Kamochis' rental car was engulfed by the slide's edge."

Still, it seemed that the Kamochis might yet come out of the incident unscathed. Yoko suffered only minor injuries, and rescuers freed her from the car in minutes. Tsuyoshi, however, was not so lucky. He was pinned under the crushed dashboard, and it took more than three hours to clear the debris, pry up the dash, and remove him from the car. He died of his injuries while trapped in the vehicle.

In the annals of freak accidents in Glacier, one poignant example stands out: In the summer of 2000, Christopher Wolk, a twenty-six-year-old man from Astoria, New York, came to the park to drive a shuttle bus for Glacier Park, Inc. Like many young people who work in the park, Wolk enjoyed the popular swimming hole at the bottom of Swiftcurrent Falls, where he went to cool off with friends on the evening of August 9. He happened to be in the path of the falling water at the exact moment when someone above the falls dislodged a large rock—later reports said it weighed twenty pounds—and no one could stop it from going over the falls. The rock hit Wolk in the head.

Other swimmers saw Wolk collapse and moved quickly to pull him out of the water, assess his injuries, and run for help. Rangers arrived, administered first aid, and called for a Mercy Flight helicopter to evacuate the young man to Benefits East Hospital in Great Falls, an emergency center with Level II trauma care. The skilled staff at the hospital worked through the evening, but by early morning it was clear that Wolk would not survive. He died quietly of massive head injuries.

None of these visitors did anything out of the ordinary to put themselves in harm's way—in fact, some of them did nothing more dangerous than sit in their own cars.

These cases all serve as reminders that a trip to a national park can come with hazards we can hardly imagine—and if our number is up, the natural forces of the universe will find a way to deliver the final blow, even if it turns out to be the kind of blow dispensed by Wile E. Coyote against the Roadrunner.

CHAPTER 9

Dropping Out of the Sky: Small Aircraft Deaths

The buzzing of small sightseeing planes and helicopters has become an all too familiar sound over Glacier National Park, but back in 1975 numerous aircraft over the park meant something far more ominous.

Residents and visitors looked up on November 4, 1975, to note at least six different planes circling over the park and recognized the aircraft of the Montana Wing of the Civil Air Patrol. This could mean only one thing: Somewhere in the park's mountainous terrain, a small aircraft had made an unscheduled and potentially disastrous landing.

While no small planes had gone down in this particular segment of the Rocky Mountain backcountry to that date, it was only a matter of time. The mountain range splits the weather patterns here into two distinct climates, with the western side of the park receiving considerably more precipitation than the eastern side, making the eastern half deceptively sunny. High winds often stir up the air currents to the east, making it particularly difficult to predict what flying through the area will be like on any given day—or even at any hour. Pilots who do not know the area and its quirks well often do their best to avoid flying over the Glacier wilderness entirely.

On Saturday, November 1, 1975, pilot Donald Donovan and passenger Kathy See flew into Kalispell from their native Coeur d'Alene, Idaho, in a single-engine Beechcraft four-seater on their way to Shelby. Donovan, a former military pilot with thousands of hours of flight experience, had a reputation for being a cautious flyer who did not take unnecessary chances. He had been a flight instructor, and he had significant experience in flying through the mountainous terrain typical of the American northwest. He carried the appropriate safety equipment of the day, including flares that he could light if his plane ever went down and he found himself in distress. Donovan must have expected an uneventful flight, albeit over a stunningly beautiful winter landscape. It was uncharacteristic of Donovan not to file a flight plan, but on this particular day he did not do so—though to get to Shelby, his shortest route would take him across the Continental Divide and directly across some of the most remote sections of the park. He refueled the plane in Kalispell and took off in the direction of the park.

People in the park would report to authorities later that they had heard a small plane flying Saturday afternoon in the area southeast of Kalispell, and one observer actually saw it. Gerald C. Burrows, search coordinator for the Montana Division of Aeronautics, would explain to reporters the next day that the pilot would seek a pass through which he could cross the Continental Divide—most likely the Marias Pass, because it was less than a mile high and directly in the flight path of the plane that residents of the area said they had heard or seen.

That was the last anyone saw of Donald Donovan, Kathy See, or the gleaming white aircraft with its smart red trim.

When the plane did not reach Shelby and authorities there contacted the Montana Aeronautics Division, heavy turbulence in the air above the southern end of the park made it virtually impossible to search effectively from the air. Burrows reluctantly limited the number of planes searching by air until Monday, when conditions improved—but when commercial flights and searchers in the area reported that they were not receiving any signal from the missing plane's emergency-locator beacon, the gravity of the situation became more and more clear. Civil Air Patrol pilots watched for Donovan's flares against the snow and ice below, but they saw nothing, an additional sign that if the plane had indeed gone down in the wilderness, no one had survived.

Nonetheless, pilots from Idaho surveyed the area near Priest River, where a hunter had said "he had heard an airplane and seen a bright flash about the time the plane disappeared," the *Idaho State Journal* reported. But as the search continued for several days and the patrols generated no clues, officials from Idaho told Burrows that they were "through unless they get some better leads."

Worse, changeable weather hampered visibility. Burrows told reporters "there was a possibility a searcher could have flown over the downed aircraft without spotting it," according to the *Idaho State Journal*. "He said snowmelt has occurred in the search area, and the splotchy effect of snowbanks could confuse aerial observers." The turbulence that had begun on

Saturday, the day the plane disappeared, continued to create hazards for searching pilots.

At the end of a fruitless week, Civil Air Patrol first lieutenant J. D. Sharp called off the search. His officers had asked every hunter or outdoorsman they met in the park and the neighboring Bob Marshall Wilderness Area to report to the Flathead County Sheriff's Office any evidence they might find that a crash may have occurred, though it seemed obvious that one had. If concrete evidence came to light, Sharp told the media, the search could resume immediately. With continued drizzle, ice forming on search planes, and the constant turbulence over the park, however, he determined that continued searching could be dangerous to the pilots.

The lack of clues fueled speculation. Sharp suggested to media that at stall speed of fifty miles per hour, Donovan's plane "could have hit with enough force to either bend tree tops or snap them off." Looking for such a clue could also be misleading, however, because high winds can create the same disturbance in the treetops. If the plane went down in the middle of a heavily forested area, it could be completely invisible from the air. If it went down in deep snow, it could have reburied itself and become totally obscured.

After November 9 reconnaissance planes stopped flying over Glacier. The air grew quiet until late spring.

On July 28, 1976, the wreckage of a single-engine airplane was discovered near Two Medicine, "scattered up and down the mountainside," said Bob Burns, park visitor protection specialist, in an interview with the *Daily Inter Lake*. It was found near Young Man Lake, leading Burns to speculate that it probably crashed on Rising Wolf Mountain, sliding down right away with the momentum of the crash or perhaps carried down later by avalanches.

About seventy feet from the plane's fuselage, searchers discovered the body of forty-five-year-old Donald Donovan. By the following day crews probing through snowbanks located the body of thirty-one-year-old Kathy See as well, buried under about six feet of snow.

The mystery of the missing plane came to a quiet close among the lingering snow of a late July day, with a flying machine in pieces on the ground.

Two Dead, Two Survived

Ten years passed before another aircraft ran into trouble in the skies over Glacier. There's a surprisingly small amount of detail available about this one, but we do know that it was a small private plane flown by a Canadian pilot and his family—and that one young woman's tenacity helped her survive and get help for her father-in-law.

When the plane went down in Glacier National Park on September 5, 1985, it carried four people: Leo and Judith Conway of Beaconsfield, Quebec; their son, James, who was twenty-nine; and his wife, Shirley Conway, a nurse in Edmonton, Alberta. The crash killed Judith immediately, while James died later in the hospital, and Leo had a broken leg and back injuries from the impact in mountainous terrain, but Shirley managed to free herself from the wreckage—despite a separated shoulder—and began a painful trek in bare feet through the northwestern Montana wilderness.

The short news article in the *Montreal Gazette* that acknowledges this heroic feat notes that Shirley walked "almost a kilometre through thick mountain brush to find help." She picked her way through what was undoubtedly a rough landscape that may have been partially covered with snow, reaching help despite the combined issues of personal grief, pain, cold, and the shock of injury and loss. The one stroke of luck in this miserable story is that the plane came down near Siyeh Bend, not far from Going-to-the-Sun Road, so Shirley did not have to make her way through miles of underbrush to find assistance.

Seven years later, on February 12, 1992, a Grumman American AA-5B aircraft went down near Logan Pass, killing two people on board: Willard and Marion Smith, both in their fifties. Remarkably, this is all that has been recorded about this plane, the circumstances of its failure, or the passengers.

To date, only one other crash in Glacier's backcountry has resulted in a death. On Saturday, April 16, 2000, pilot Dale Laird, who was forty-two at the time, began a solo flight from Polson, Montana, to Lethbridge, Alberta, a route that would take him over Glacier Park. The Maule model M-5-210C aircraft's registration listed Laird as a resident of Wasila, Alaska, but he had been living in the Plains area of western Montana most recently. Laird filed a visual flight plan with the FAA, meaning that he planned to navigate through the park based on what he could actually see from the air, using visual references to the ground, other aircraft, and any obstructions.

When he failed to arrive at Lethbridge at the time he had specified, the airport moved quickly to report him missing. Radar records showed that Laird's plane had disappeared from the radar in the Many Glacier region of the park, where ice and snow still covered most of the ground. A search began in that area on the day the plane vanished and continued into a third day on Tuesday, focusing on the high country and involving at least six aircraft, including a helicopter from Malmstrom Air Force Base at Great Falls, and members of the Montana Civil Air Patrol. Canadian pilots joined the search as well, patrolling above the border in case the plane had managed to come that far.

Finally, on Wednesday, April 19, Ray Sanders of the Montana Aeronautics Division office in Kalispell reported that the helicopter pilot and crew had discovered the wreckage of Laird's plane, about two miles northwest of Many Glacier near Kennedy Lake, north of Mount Henkel (a peak that tops out at 8,770 feet). The crew of the helicopter confirmed that Laird had died in the crash.

Today, the sound of small planes and helicopters over Glacier National Park has become so ubiquitous that people barely look up when they hear the buzz of a motor or the whirring of a helicopter's rotors. As many as six different flightseeing companies frequent the skies above the park, bringing tourists the most expansive views possible of the Lewis and Livingston ranges of the Rocky Mountains and the adjacent Great Bear Wilderness Area, Flathead National Forest, and Lewis and Clark National Forest. The air above this park may be tricky to navigate, but these pilots are proud of their safety records and their ability to determine the best routes for the most spectacular sights. Seeing the park from the air remains one of the once-in-a-lifetime opportunities people embrace when then come to this wild place—and they return safely to the ground on a daily basis.

CHAPTER 10

The Last Hopeless Act: Suicides

IN THE MOST REMOTE CORNER OF GLACIER NATIONAL Park, past the Polebridge Ranger Station and at the end of the only road in the northwestern part of the park—a road the park closed altogether in winter—Ranger William B. McAfee spent quiet day after quiet day alone in the Kishenehn Ranger Station in the Kintla Lake district.

Back in 1926, no sport utility vehicles existed to brave the rough, snow-covered road, and the only human contact the ranger could look forward to was a person or two he might meet when he trekked out to the Trail Creek post office for his mail. He could not even depend on this on a daily basis, however, as winter storms and deep snow could make his route impassable. McAfee's days would be spent in solitude, performing his backcountry duties in the bitter cold of a Montana winter, watching the frozen landscape, and hoping for the slightest change to break the perpetual stillness.

Perhaps it's no wonder that on February 9, at the icy season's nadir, Ranger McAfee chose to end his life by shooting himself through the head.

Two homesteaders named Peterson found him when they thought to check on the ranger after he did not make his daily trip to the post office for several days. They most likely snowshoed up to the station on Tuesday of that week and found McAfee's body "lying in the snow between his cabin and the stable behind a building, with a bullet hole through the head, just back of the ears," according to the *Independent Record*. His gun lay nearby, with just one .38-caliber bullet discharged, and no tracks led to or from the body other than McAfee's own. Coroner Campbell determined that it was a clear case of suicide.

"McAfee, who was an ex-service man, had been heard to complain of ill health," the paper reported. "He had frequently remarked that the loneliness of his station was getting the better of him, a condition which the park officials were not aware of."

Too stoic to admit to the weaknesses of isolation and possibly in the throes of depression, McAfee saw suicide as his most practical way out of his unhappiness. He was the first of seven people who are known to have taken their own lives in this park, perhaps choosing the park's spectacular scenery as the last place they would see at the moment they pulled the trigger.

A Disturbing Upward Trend

Suicides in national parks happen frequently enough that the National Park Service and the Centers for Disease Control joined forces in 2010 to look closely at the phenomenon, to determine what attracted so many people—a total of 286 in eight-four parks from 2003 to 2009—to attempt to take their own lives in the parks. Of these attempts, 68 percent (194) were successful, resulting in the person's death.

The study discovered that firearms and falls—leaps from a high precipice or bridge, or speeding over a cliff in a motor vehicle or on a mountain bike—were the most prevalent methods tried for ending one's own life. Consistent with patterns of suicide throughout the country in any venue, 83 percent of the attempts were by men. (In Glacier, all seven successful suicides were male.)

During the period examined by the study, the National Park Service averaged twenty-eight suicides and thirteen attempted suicides each year. (Glacier National Park only had one successful suicide in this period, in the summer of 2008.) These figures are high enough for park service officials to consider the actions that could be taken to prevent such events, or at least to spot people who may have come to a park for the express purpose of taking their own lives.

With millions of visitors coming to the parks every year and the likelihood that suicidal people will not seek out contact with others when they arrive for this purpose, how can parks take steps to keep such events from occurring? If you're asking that question as you read this, you are not alone. Andrew Gulliford of the *High Country News* posed exactly that inquiry. "How does one prevent such deaths?" he asked. "Do we need to erect traffic barriers at every lookout point or install safety nets at every cliff? At Colorado National Monument, for example, depressed people have chosen to ride their mountain bikes right over sheer cliffs."

Barriers and restrictions to access are indeed one of the strategies the CDC suggested as a result of its study, but its main recommendation probably will have the greater effect: Parks should collaborate with community prevention programs "to gain increased access to resources, guidance, and training."

Even beyond the opportunity to save lives and help suicidal individuals see that there are other ways to improve their circumstances, the parks have a reality to contend with as well: Putting park resources toward the process of searching for a suicide victim in the remote backcountry, pulling a smashed vehicle out of a canyon, or removing a body from the bottom of a cliff can all put additional lives in danger—and these operations can be extraordinarily expensive. The CDC report notes that one such search for a missing person who had killed himself cost a park nearly two hundred thousand dollars. It may seem unspeakably mercenary to see such an event in these terms, but the high cost of search and rescue operations is a fact of life in national parks, where budgets are strained beyond their ability to cover daily expenses and federal funding gets tighter every year.

Killing Yourself at a Cost

Bruce Colburn came to Glacier National Park in 2008 from Reading, Pennsylvania, for what appeared to be a backcountry adventure. He flew into Glacier Park International Airport on October 7, spent the night in a hotel, and got a ride to the park from a hotel employee. On October 8 he told a park ranger he planned to hike into the wilderness. He was well equipped for some serious hiking with a new backpack and tent, and he had told his family he would be gone for anywhere from a week to nearly a month.

The ranger told him that he needed a permit to camp overnight in the backcountry, but Colburn decided against filling out the paperwork. He spent the night where he did not need a permit, in his new tent at Kintla Lake Campground, and was one of only a handful of campers this late in the season.

The next morning, on October 9, Colburn—who until recently had been president and CEO of a bill collection service for hospitals and health clinics—headed out along Kintla Lake. That was the last anyone saw of him.

Weeks passed. Colburn had told the hotel employee that he would be in contact with him "in a couple of weeks," when he returned from his backpacking trip. He left his luggage and other belongings at the hotel, but never returned to retrieve them.

On October 23, when this acquaintance had not yet heard from Colburn, he called the park and reported him missing. The search for the Pennsylvania businessman began in the Kintla and Bowman Lake drainages, with some searchers focusing on Goat Haunt, in the northernmost part of the park along the Canadian border. Family members warned the park rangers that they knew Colburn was carrying a handgun, a .40-caliber Beretta.

Search and rescue crews were already baffled that fall by the disappearance of Yi-Jien Hwa in August (see chapter 5) and their failure to find him, so they were perhaps even more eager than usual to find Colburn. More than thirty people scoured the backcountry, from park rangers to US Border Patrol agents, as well as Flathead County's expert search and rescue teams. Even the FBI played a role in the search.

The familiar sound of small planes and helicopters broke the north country silence in the otherwise remote area in the Boundary Mountains.

Six days later, on October 29, searchers saw a backpack near the head of Kintla Lake. "That was relayed to the aerial searchers, and the body was spotted from the air as a result of locating the pack," park spokesperson Amy Vanderbilt told the *Daily Inter Lake*.

Colburn, who was fifty-three, took his life with a single gunshot to the chest. Searchers discovered his body several hundred yards above the trail, near Kintla Lake.

As news of his death spread from Montana to Pennsylvania, only a hint or two of Colburn's motivation came to light. When he came to Glacier, he was unemployed, and when Flathead County Undersheriff Pete Wingert contacted his former employer, the staff confirmed only that he was no longer with the company. "All I was told is he was laid off," Wingert told the *Independent Record* on October 31. No other details appeared in the media, nor would such personal facts be any of our business under normal circumstances—but Colburn chose to commit suicide in a national park, causing a prolonged, taxpayer-funded search for his remains. Chances are that some of these taxpayers feel that they are owed some kind of explanation.

Yet one of the most disquieting things about suicides in the national parks is how little we know about what drove the victims to take their own lives. Such was the case with Paul E. Jones, an electrician on the Anaconda Aluminum Company potline expansion in the park in 1965, who was found near Avalanche Campground on the Going-to-the-Sun Road, lying behind his parked pickup truck with his .22 pistol by his side. The unlucky soul who found him was road foreman Claude Tesmer, accompanied by his crew as they started their workday on May 11, 1965, just before eight a.m. Beyond an estimate of the time of death—sometime between ten p.m. and midnight the night before—the only additional detail we know is that Jones left a note to his wife, Bessie.

In the cases of twenty-nine-year-old Larry Jones (presumably no relation to Paul), who shot himself in the Apgar picnic area in 1968, and Peter Soderlund, twenty-five, found asphyxiated near Packers Roost in April 1986, the news of each death managed to stay out of the mainstream media. Likewise, coverage of the self-inflicted death of a man from Virginia Beach, Virginia, in March 2015 contained only the fact of his death and the manner in which it took place, but no name or other identification. He was found by three visitors who discovered him one morning, slumped over the steering wheel of his vehicle about a mile from the foot of Lake McDonald.

The park and law enforcement exercised admirable discretion around the apparent suicide of thirty-year-old Clinton Croff, a well-known Native American singer and dancer from Browning, when the young man was "reportedly involved in altercations near road construction traffic on the road into the Two Medicine Valley" on a Thursday morning in late July 2010. When called for assistance, park rangers responded and found Croff "combative and suffering from multiple wounds." The rangers began emergency medical treatment, and when Croff collapsed, they administered CPR and called for an ALERT helicopter to transport him to a hospital. By the time the air ambulance arrived, however, Croff's life had ended.

Police said no more publicly about the incident, even after the autopsy. The *Native American Times* noted several weeks later that the FBI's Salt Lake City office, which was investigating the incident to provide an impartial third-party opinion, closed the case without filing charges against any individual. The national park quietly listed the death as a suicide, while friends in Browning "said they've been told an agitated Croff committed suicide inside his car, by way of multiple self-inflicted stab wounds, but park officials would not confirm those details," according to Michael Jamison, reporting for the *Missoulian*.

Given the nature of each of these incidents, the majority of which happen when the victim is alone, it can be hard to fathom the CDC's statement that "each death represents a preventable event in a public place."

In the next breath the CDC's report goes on to say, "Park rangers have intervened to prevent suicides; however, their ability to dissuade suicidal visitors is limited. Training programs for park rangers should consider factors such as awareness of any ability to connect to local community prevention programs for information and guidance, and the typically short duration that park rangers interact with visitors . . . Enhanced training that focuses on the ability to recognize the signs and symptoms of suicidal behavior, provides strategies for reaching out to persons with problems, and improves the understanding of available treatment might prove useful."

In many parks, rangers are trained in suicide prevention, and some parks even teach their employees to keep an eye out for notes taped to steering wheels in empty cars. Parks do what they can to keep these incidents from taking place, but when a person chooses to make a last desperate gesture in one of the most glorious places in the country, there may be nothing anyone can do to stop him.

CHAPTER 11

Deathly Cold:
Dying of Exposure

IN THE DEAD OF WINTER IN 1913, THREE YEARS AFTER Glacier became a national park, it took an uncommon level of determination to be a backcountry ranger in this ice-encased, windswept corner of Montana. Every move from one station to another required skis or snowshoes, multiple layers of clothing, backpacks loaded with supplies, and finely honed wilderness survival skills that included the ability to "siwash," or sleep outside in the bitter cold without a tent.

Four men patrolled the perimeter of the park in those days, rangers who tramped every day through forests and across frozen tundra, trudging in pairs or as a group to the next homesteader's cabin or official park ranger station. Norton Pearl did us the supreme courtesy of recording his explorations in his diaries, which his daughter, Leslie Lee, compiled in the fascinating book *Backcountry Ranger in Glacier National Park, 1910-1913*. He broke trail in lockstep with fellow ranger Joe Prince and park superintendent James L. Galen, while Kootenay Brown and the pessimistically named Death-on-the-Trail Reynolds covered the western side of the park. Ranger Reynolds described his first perimeter patrol as one "which no man can make."

In the end, the most experienced ranger became the least able to complete the trek.

In that patrol, on January 9, 1913, Pearl and Galen took their cues from Joe Prince, a well-respected mountain man with finely honed winter survival skills. He directed his comrades to a shortcut that would get them from Two Medicine to St. Mary in less time, minimizing their exposure to the extreme cold and the winds that tore at their clothes and blinded their eyes with drifting snow.

Prince was the ranger at Cut Bank, so if he said the shortcut was a good one, Pearl and Galen were ready to believe him. Sure enough, the two of them plodded along together into St. Mary in less time than they could have imagined. They noted that Prince had begun to lag behind, but the potential hazards of this did not occur to them right away, because the rugged ranger knew the terrain so well and understood the dangers of lingering too long in the cold. When he did not arrive at St. Mary by nightfall, they assumed that he had decided to siwash in the wilderness and continue in the morning.

Morning came, but Prince did not arrive. Pearl saw that he had no choice but to head back across the shortcut toward Two Medicine to see where his colleague may have run into trouble, hoping that Prince had built himself a wind block with brush or sticks to keep himself sheltered overnight. He watched the route for any kind of structure that would tell him where Prince might have spent the frosty hours in the dark.

Instead, he found Prince's rigid body, huddled on the park boundary line in the snow. An unopened can of sardines sat next to him, as did a pair of sheepskin boots.

"Poor Old Prince," Pearl wrote later that day in his diary, once he was back at St. Mary. "He cashed in last night . . . frozen and cold in the snow."

Remarkably, Joe Prince was the only one of the original four rangers who died of exposure in those early days on patrol. What may have triggered this mountain man's reflex to sit down in the snow and await death can be known only to him, but his action served as a warning to the others: Patrolling on the edge of the park can push even the strongest and most experienced ranger over the edge into eternity.

Summer Exposure

Most visitors and staff members in Glacier are not required to cross the park's terrain in the dead of January, but even the summer months can bring tumultuous conditions that make overnights in the backcountry a tricky experience. The culprit here is the Continental Divide, the line from the Bering Strait in Alaska to the Strait of Magellan at the southern tip of South America, forming the division of watersheds for the entire continent. On the eastern side of the divide, water from rain, melting snow, and weather events flows down the Rocky Mountains and across the continent toward the Atlantic Ocean. On the western side, water flows down toward the Pacific Ocean.

While North America has a number of dividing lines that change the direction of watersheds, the Continental Divide is unique because of its high elevation. For the most part, the line follows the highest parts of the Rocky Mountains and the Andes, entering Glacier National Park along the US/Canadian border between Glacier and Waterton Lakes National Park. From here it bisects Glacier, creating a line along which two distinct weather patterns churn against one another to produce volatile conditions just about any time of year. From the Pacific side, warm, moist air climbs the mountains toward the divide. From the Atlantic side, the air climbing the mountainsides is colder and drier. At the clash of these two systems, the dry air robs the wetter air of its moisture, and it falls as precipitation—in most years as much as one hundred inches of rain and snow can fall along the divide. The snowpack up here can be as deep as sixteen feet—which is why parts of Going-to-the-Sun Road are closed for the duration of the winter. Keeping up with removal of that much snow would take resources the park is never likely to receive.

What does this mean for visitors? If you're planning to hike out into the backcountry at any time of year, you must be prepared for snowfields, deep snow, ice, and the bitterest kind of cold, combining dry winds with damp air to create muscle-chilling wintriness even in the middle of summer.

So in August 1925, when the camp cook at Sprague Creek realized that Mr. and Mrs. J. B. Wheeler's campsite had gone untouched for a week, rangers knew that they might be looking for two people who had succumbed to freezing temperatures. They began their search for the retired couple from Whitefish by following the trail to Snyder Lake at the Sperry chalets, where the couple had told others they planned to hike on their way to Lake Ellen Wilson. They purchased food supplies at Sperry for a two-day trip.

Two search parties and one trail crew spent a week scouring trails looking for the couple, finally fanning out into a larger area including Little St. Mary, in case the Wheelers had ventured that far off their intended route. They knew that Wheeler had worked for the park service on construction of Sprague Camp and on the road near Lake McDonald the previous season, so he had a greater familiarity than most visitors would with the structure of the park and its many attractions—and, they hoped, its hazards as well.

On September 1, ten days after the search began and eighteen days after the Wheelers had last been seen at Sperry chalets, Ranger J. B. Fleming discovered their bodies about fifteen yards off the trail at Lincoln Pass. The couple had hiked about a mile and a half above Sperry chalets when a snowstorm hit, dropping a foot of snow on the area and socking in the hikers. Well provisioned for two days of hiking and otherwise unprepared for this kind of onslaught, the Wheelers took cover under a shelving rock, but their attempt to build a fire failed, and the drop in temperature and the thick, heavy precipitation proved too much for them.

"In the course of his employment [Wheeler] had worked upon the very trail near which he lost his life," the *Lethbridge Herald* in Alberta, Canada, reported in its coverage of the incident.

Some Who Wander Are Lost

The discovery of the body of Bishop William F. Faber, the seventy-four-year-old presiding head of the Episcopal Diocese of Montana, put to rest considerable speculation about where the elderly gentleman had gone when he left the Two Medicine chalets for a pleasant hike before dinner four days earlier, on July 20, 1934.

Young Glenn Johnston, the seven-year-old son of the Two Medicine boat captain, saw the elderly bishop walk up a trail behind the boathouse that Friday night, making the boy the last person to see Bishop Faber alive. The clergyman had come to Glacier every year for the last twenty years to hike the trails and enjoy the scenery, and just a few days before, he had gone with a group of friends to hike up Mount Henry, a summit of 8,848 feet. Short and sturdy, the bishop felt comfortable in the park—but just recently, friends had noticed that he seemed to be more confused than in years past, and directions and distances had become something of a jumble for him.

Four days of searching led Ranger Clyde Fauley to find Bishop Faber in Paradise Creek, his body lying against a log where he apparently slipped or stumbled as he walked down the stream. After surveying the scene and determining that the bishop still carried his money and other property, park officials speculated that the elderly man had become confused in the woods and "after wandering for two or three hours, decided to walk down the creek until he came to Two Medicine lake, a trail or some landmark which he might recognize," the Associated Press wrote on the evening the bishop was found. "It was thought that the bishop entered the stream, the banks of which are steep in places, as a final means of finding his way back to the point he left for a hike before dinner."

He fell into just two feet of water in the creek, but like all streams in the park, this one was fed by "melting glaciers and snow high in the towering mountains," making it only a few degrees warmer than ice. In the ensuing three days, frigid overnight temperatures caused water to freeze in the bottoms of boats on Two Medicine Lake. This was not the weather the bishop, who hailed originally from the Buffalo, New York, area, would be accustomed to in the middle of July.

County Coroner M. A. O'Neil of Cut Bank noted that the body's upper portion was not submerged or even wet, so the cause of death had to be exposure, perhaps accompanied by the shock of the fall. Searchers had feared that the bishop had drowned and been washed away in a rushing stream. While finding him dead did not give his story a happy ending, it did give the diocese the opportunity to bring closure to his parish and honor the man's passing in the most dignified way, with an appropriate funeral.

Many decades would pass before another park visitor would perish in the park strictly because of the cold, and even that one came about simply because a rescue took longer than anticipated.

The hike to Grinnell Glacier, one of the most popular in the park, generally is not seen as especially hazardous. Most people take the shuttle boats across Swiftcurrent Lake and Lake Josephine, leaving about 3.6 miles of hiking—much of it uphill—to reach Grinnell Lake and the foot of Grinnell Glacier, crossing a marshy area on a boardwalk, an expansive field of wildflowers, areas frequented by mountain goats and bighorn sheep, and stretches of grizzly country before you reach the glacier. "In years past rangers would lead hikes out onto the glacier itself," the website Hikingin Glacier.com notes. "However, as a result of its retreat in recent years, rangers no longer take groups out onto the ice.

The park does allow visitors to venture out onto the glacier, but they highly recommend that you don't go alone, or go too far. It's especially dangerous when there's fresh snow on the ground, which can hide deep crevasses." Here is the story of one person who did not have this very good advice before he ventured out alone on the glacier.

Howard Frederick Cohn, a forty-six-year-old visitor from Columbia, Maryland, and three other hikers, including Cohn's wife, Debbie, made the trek out to Grinnell Glacier on July 27, 2004. Called "an outdoorsman who craved a challenge" by the *Howard County Times* in Maryland, Cohn loved to hike in any weather, and the vacations he took with his wife and friends usually included cross-country skiing or hiking in places like the White Mountains in New Hampshire or the Adirondack Mountains in northern New York state. They had even been to Glacier fourteen years before, so Cohn had a good idea what kinds of activities he wanted to enjoy on this second visit.

Like many hikers, Cohn must have been taken with the novelty of hiking on ice in the middle of summer, so he decided to make a quick trip out onto the glacier itself—a move his three companions declined to take. He left them at the edge of the glacier and headed out at about three p.m. for a close-up look at this natural wonder.

When thirty minutes had passed and Cohn had not returned, his friends proceeded carefully onto the ice to look for him. They did not see him at first, but in a few minutes they heard him calling for help. Cohn had taken a wrong step and slid thirty-five feet down into a glacial crevasse. Without appropriate ice climbing gear, he could not get out.

Luckily, a ranger was nearby leading a tour, and he radioed for help. A rescue team arrived quickly from Many Glacier and found Cohn wedged below them but talkative, and they set to work to free him from the crack. They discovered soon enough that three feet of snow had come down on top of Cohn, and that the crevasse was a mere eighteen inches wide, so he was wedged into place and unable to move much. The rescuers knew what this meant: Cohn had no way to keep warm as they worked to free him. His body temperature began to drop, and he grew quiet over the course of the four-hour process to pull him out of the crevasse.

Finally, at about eight p.m., the rescuers got Cohn back to the surface. They began CPR until an ALERT helicopter arrived to fly him to Kalispell Regional Medical Center, where doctors worked to restore his body temperature to normal before it became clear that the man had slipped beyond their help. Cohn was pronounced dead from "multiple system trauma," with head, chest, and abdominal injuries in addition to hypothermia.

Perhaps stories like these have helped keep any other hikers from dying of exposure in Glacier since 2004, by reminding them not to walk out into the park's wilderness areas without all of the emergency gear they can carry, from extra clothing to fire-starting tools, ropes, pulleys, crampons, and a wide range of other equipment. You may feel a little silly packing as if you plan to climb a mountain when you're out for a woodland stroll, but in the risky terrain at Glacier, it's better to be ready for any eventuality than to march out into the backcountry without the one piece of gear that could save your life.

CHAPTER 12

Murder Most Expedient: The Volkswagen Van and the Newlywed Case

IN A VINTAGE VOLKSWAGEN VAN OUTFITTED FOR CAMPING, Frederick H. Pongrace set out from Washington, D.C., in early July 1983 to explore the country. He had just been discharged from the US Coast Guard on June 30, with which he helped conduct research on chemical and oil spills in the ocean and determine their effect on the environment, so he was ready for some unstructured recreational time before starting a new job in Seattle, Washington. Pongrace planned an itinerary that would take him through a range of national parks, including some in Minnesota and other states, culminating in a trip to Glacier.

On Thursday, July 14, 1983, at about ten thirty a.m., a group of tourists stepped up to the edge of Crystal Point in Glacier to take some photos of Heaven's Peak. They looked down one hundred ninety feet to the bottom of the sheer drop-off inches from their feet . . . and they saw a body. Somehow, Frederick Pongrace—a man exercising his wanderlust and exploring America's most beautiful places on the way to start a new life—ended up dead at the foot of a rock wall.

"An autopsy showed Mr. Pongrace died from the fall," said park ranger Jerry Bell in an interview with the *Grosse Point News* in Michigan, where Frederick's parents lived. "He wasn't dead before he went over the cliff."

Some of the evidence proved to be hard to come by at first, Bell told the *Missoulian* thirty years later. Four abdominal wounds didn't look like they could have happened in the fall, but an inch and a half of rain had fallen overnight while Pongrace's body lay at the bottom of the cliff, so blood and other clues had washed away. It took some time before the medical examiner identified the cuts as stab wounds.

How exactly had this young man died, and why? The answer serves as a cautionary tale for all road-trippers across the country, a reminder that being a Good Samaritan to peculiar strangers can end in the worst possible way.

About sixty miles east of Glacier National Park, Pongrace spotted a hitchhiker walking with a black Labrador retriever along the side of the road. Pongrace picked the man up, and they apparently became friends in short order. "They spent the night in a campground," Frederick's father, Otto Pongrace, told the newspaper, "but were asked to leave the next day because the dog was causing trouble. The owner of the camp said Fred could stay, but he left with the hitchhiker."

Later, investigators learned that this clash happened at the Shady Grove Campground outside of Cut Bank. Not only had the dog been a problem, but the hitchhiker had pulled a knife on other campers as well, leading the owner to throw him out of the camp. The camp owner told investigators later that Pongrace was upset that he refused to allow the hitch-hiker to stay. "[Pongrace] told the hitchhiker, 'I brought you here. I'll see you get out,'" Bell related to reporters. "He was so upset he called the police about the camp owner." Police received calls at seven thirty a.m. and three p.m. from Pongrace on Wednesday, July 13, the first one definitely having to do with the camp owner. The second call, however, may have been made when Pongrace discovered he was traveling with a thief.

That's when things started to go wrong. "We believe that my son discovered the hitchhiker was wanted for a robbery in Canada, and tried to call the police," Otto Pongrace continued. "The next thing you know, his body was found at the bottom of a cliff." His van and money—about seven hundred dollars in cash, plus another thousand dollars in traveler's checks—were gone. The car keys were missing as well.

Frederick's identification was not on his body, but he still had the registration for the van in a billfold. Park rangers called Frederick's sister, who was listed as a co-owner of the van, and got a positive identification of the deceased from her.

"He wasn't dressed for hiking," Otto said. "My son was very meticulous and wouldn't walk off and leave the van unlocked. We know it was foul play."

Working with the FBI and local law enforcement, Bell put out an all-points bulletin on the van, and the team began to piece together the story from there.

They received a report that the hitchhiker, a man named Scott David Steel, had spent the next night in the van outside Ronan, miring the vehicle in mud and calling a tow truck when he couldn't pull it out. When the truck arrived, the hitchhiker had no money, so he gave the driver Pongrace's camera. This raised plenty of red flags for the truck driver, so he called the police and reported this behavior as suspicious.

With a name in hand, Bell and the FBI could narrow the search. Customs agents on the US/Canadian border reported that Steel and his dog had crossed into the country from Canada on the day before he hooked up with Pongrace. The agents had examined the contents of his backpack and noted that his identification said he lived in California. "They didn't take his name," Ranger Bell told reporters. "They had no reason to. We later found out he had robbed someone in Canada."

According to police in Canada, the suspect had befriended some people in a bar in Alberta, and they had invited him back to their home for beers and more conversation. He accepted, went to their house, drank their beer, and then took the keys to one man's truck and stole his wallet out of the front seat. "He locked the keys in the truck and took off," said Bell. "He really treats people who befriend him real nice."

Reports came in from Wolf Point and from Havre as well, including another robbery, this one of money from another man who had been nice enough to give the hitchhiker a ride.

As more clues to Steel's whereabouts came in, the manhunt stretched west and southward toward California. Checkpoints at the state border did not turn up anyone matching Steel's description, but the investigation got another stroke of luck a few days later when police in Los Angeles got a report that people were trying to break into a Volkswagen van matching the description of Pongrace's vehicle. Police responded quickly enough to keep the evidence in the van intact: bloodstains in the backseat and rear areas of the van, as well as on the seat belt. They also found a piece of paper with a phone number on it—and when they called the number, they discovered Steel's sister, who was training to be a police officer. She turned out to be more than helpful in the investigation, providing access to her residence for a search. Police found Pongrace's belongings in the possessions Steel had brought into the house.

Investigators had the proof they needed, but they could not find Steel. Months went by with no additional leads.

"Golly, it must have been six months, seven months, something like that," said Bell in the *Missoulian* in 2013, on the thirty-year anniversary of this murder. "I get a call from St. George, Utah, that they picked up this guy."

Steel was transferred to Missoula, where he finally faced a jury for the murder of Frederick Pongrace. Despite an argument by the defense that Steel may have simply stolen the van when Pongrace didn't return from a hike, the four-day trial and four hours of jury deliberations ended in a conviction. He was sentenced to life in prison.

Sixteen years later Steel received parole and moved to the Twin Falls, Idaho, area in 2000. After three years there, Steel "absconded from supervision" and ran to Mexico, where he lived for another six years, according to the US Marshals website. Said US Marshal Patrick E. McDonald in a prepared statement, "With the help of the Mexican Immigration officials and the US Marshals using their international resources, this criminal was arrested in Mexico after 6 years on the lamb [*sic*]. Even if you run to Mexico, but have a persistent Deputy US Marshal on your trail, the long arm of the law will get you one day."

Steel was returned to Los Angeles, served time for the parole violation, and was released again in 2010. He appears to have maintained a low profile since then.

THE HONEYMOON MURDER

Thirty years passed before Glacier saw another death suspicious enough to warrant an extended investigation. This one rose to national consciousness as its players—a couple married just eight days—displayed the most notorious "second thoughts" about marriage ever seen in the national park system.

Close friends of Cody Lee Johnson, who was twenty-five in 2013, told him that his upcoming marriage to twenty-two-year-old Jordan Linn Graham looked to them to be a bad idea. "Their interaction with each other, it didn't seem like a happy, loving relationship that you would normally see," groomsman Cameron Frederickson told reporter Alice Miller at the *Missoulian*. "It was just very awkward, I guess. She was just very distant and reserved."

Johnson and Graham were married on June 29, 2013, and he was expected back at work on July 8. When Johnson did not come to work at Nomad Global Communications Systems in Kalispell on that Monday, however, his coworkers called his family, and his uncle called the police. Johnson was nowhere to be found. Law enforcement began their search, interviewing Jordan Graham on July 9 to determine where Johnson might have gone.

Graham told FBI special agent Steven Liss that she and Johnson had gone to dinner with friends on the night of July 7 and that "during the drive home, Johnson received a cell phone call that caused him to be upset," according to the official affidavit Liss wrote about his interview with Graham. She told the agent that when they arrived home, she realized that her cell phone needed charging and that her charger was at "another location." She said she took the car and drove to this location to retrieve her charger, and while she was out, Johnson texted her to say that he was going out with a friend from out of town.

"When Graham arrived at the house she advised she saw a dark colored car pulling out of the driveway," the affidavit continued. "Graham stated she is sure Johnson was in the dark car."

When asked to produce Johnson's text, Graham told the agent that "she and Johnson routinely delete their text messages; thus she was unable to produce the above-referenced text for viewing."

Graham's story began to unravel almost as soon as she had spoken. Liss went on to interview Kimberly Martinez, Graham's maid of honor, who said that Graham had texted her on the evening of July 7, saying that she was about to talk to Johnson about her "second thoughts" about marrying him. When Martinez responded, "I'll pray for you guys," Graham came back with, "But dead serious if u don't hear from me at all again tonight, something happened."

Kalispell police issued a news release saying that Johnson "was believed to have left his home with some unidentified friends in a black car headed toward Hungry Horse and

West Glacier." Graham told police that the car had Washington state license plates.

The affidavit next notes that on Wednesday, July 10, Graham received an e-mail from an unidentified person, who said that Johnson "had left with three friends, went hiking, had fallen, was dead, and the search should be called off." Months later Agent Liss told the *Missoulian* that the FBI had traced the e-mail account back to Stephen Rutledge, Jordan Graham's stepfather, and that it was sent from an account created that day.

On Thursday, July 11, a park ranger responded to a dispatch coming from the Lake McDonald Camp Store. It seemed that a visitor had discovered a dead body within the park. Perhaps you can imagine the ranger's reaction when the "visitor" turned out to be Jordan Graham! Graham reported that she had found a body below the Loop, a trail below the slingshot turn at a popular viewpoint on Going-to-the-Sun Road. Rangers moved quickly to recover the body, calling on a specialized rescue team from Parks Canada to remove the remains from the bottom of the cliff, two hundred feet below the trail. It didn't take long to identify the body as Cody Lee Johnson.

The ranger told Graham that he thought it was odd that she was the one who found the body. Graham told him, "It was a place he wanted to see before he died. He would come up here with friends to drive fast when his friends were visiting from out of state."

The search story ends here, but the investigation into Johnson's death became focused on one suspect.

On Tuesday, July 16, in her third interview with police since Johnson's disappearance, Jordan Graham admitted that she had lied to investigators, and she confessed to pushing Johnson over the cliff. She told Agent Liss that she and her husband had quarreled and then decided to go to Glacier to hike. They continued to argue in the car on the way to the Loop, and as they began their hike, the argument intensified. "At one point in time during their arguing, Graham turned and began to walk away. She stated Johnson grabbed her by the arm. Graham turned and removed Johnson's hand from her arm . . . Graham stated that she could have just walked away, but due to her anger, she pushed Johnson with both hands in the back and as a result, he fell face first off the cliff."

Even with this confession in hand, for weeks following the discovery of Johnson's body investigating organizations went almost completely silent. The FBI, which leads the investigation of any major case that takes place on federal land, told the media nothing except that the case was still open—not even that they had received a confession from Graham. "We do not have a projected completion date, as each case is unique and requires thorough investigation," FBI spokesperson Patsy Speelman wrote in an e-mail to the *Missoulian*.

Finally, on September 9, police arrested Graham and charged her with second-degree murder. Despite the protestations of prosecuting attorneys, Graham was released to her parents' home under house arrest, and US Magistrate Judge Jeremiah Lynch ordered that she "undergo mental health evaluation and complete any recommended treatment."

The case then went before a grand jury, which returned an indictment on October 4, escalating the charges to first-degree murder—despite her defense attorney's insistence that she acted in self-defense—with the lesser charges of second-degree murder and making false statements.

Over the next several months, as the media spiraled this story up to the national level in anticipation of the trial, the prosecution revealed all manner of sordid details. The *New York Daily News* reported that Graham may have blind-folded Johnson before pushing him off the cliff, and the *Missoulian* confirmed that a piece of cloth found in the creek near Johnson's body contained six human hairs and other "trace evidence." Court documents suggested that Graham had threatened to kill her mother and stepfather just a few weeks before she pushed Johnson, and that these statements "should be admitted to negate innocent intent and demonstrate the likelihood that the defendant did act with the requisite intent in the charged case." The prosecution said it had evidence that Graham had made up "allegations of abuse from previous relationships" as a factor in her rash actions against her husband.

The trial finally commenced in December, and by the time all the evidence had been presented, Graham and her defense attorneys saw the handwriting on the wall. Just before closing arguments they offered a guilty plea to second-degree murder that would prevent the case from going to a jury for deliberation on the first-degree murder charge, which would carry a much longer sentence. The prosecution and US District Judge John Molloy accepted Graham's plea and dropped the charges of premeditated first-degree murder and making false statements. The defense attorneys requested a ten-year sentence as part of the plea deal.

When the sentencing hearing came in March 2014, the judge had other ideas. Jordan Graham received a sentence of 365 months in prison—that's thirty years and five months—without the possibility of parole. Judge Molloy said at the time of sentencing that he did not believe that Graham showed any remorse for what she had done—a statement that turned out to be just the fodder her defense team needed to file an appeal a month later, saying the court had reneged on the terms of her guilty plea by inflicting a sentence reserved for first-degree murder convictions. The defense presented its appeal in the Ninth Circuit Court of Appeals in October 2014, and the prosecution responded in late January 2015. In November 2015 the appeals court upheld Graham's sentence, and she continues to serve her 365 months in prison.

CHAPTER 13

Missing:
Presumed Dead

THEIR STORIES HAVE BEEN TOLD AND RETOLD IN BOOKS, IN magazine and newspaper articles, and on blogs and websites, but to this day, no new clues have ever revealed what happened to seven men who hiked off into the Glacier wilderness and were never seen again.

It's hard to call one story more mysterious than another, as they all end the same way—in that they do not end at all. In every case a man (or in one case, two brothers) walked off on a trail to discover some area of the park as part of a strenuous summer's exploration or a day's desire for solitude. In every case they vanished, and no final understanding of their fate ever emerged.

Take, for example, the complicated case of Joseph and William Whitehead, two young men who were twenty-nine and twenty-two at the time of their disappearance. In the summer of 1924, they came to Glacier National Park together for a week of trekking through the forests and along the mountain ridges. Joseph was on vacation from his job as an engineer for the Universal Battery Company in Chicago, and William was enrolled at the Massachusetts Institute of Technology. Upstanding men in every part of their lives, they wrote at least one long letter to their mother, Dora White-head, during their trip out west, assuring her that they were taking every precaution to come home safely. "We are enjoying ourselves very much and taking no chances of injuring ourselves," Joseph wrote in his last letter to his mother on August 20, 1924. "Don't worry, mother, we won't go into any danger."

No one wants their last written words to be proved so completely wrong, as these were just a few days later. On August 24 Joseph and William walked out of Granite Park Chalet to begin a twenty-mile hike to the Lewis Hotel at Lake McDonald, where they would board a train for home. Other hikers reported that they saw the two young men halfway along their hiking route, just about ten miles distant from the Lewis Hotel, dressed in knickers, smiling and enjoying the gorgeous scenery. They had told people in the park that they planned to fish along their route.

Where in heaven and earth they may have ended up after that remains anyone's guess.

When the Whiteheads didn't get off the train on September 1 to meet their mother—a week after they were supposed to board the train at Lake McDonald—she immediately got in touch with authorities. An exhaustive search of the park began, one that involved every resource the area could provide. "Thirteen rangers, two famous Indian Guides and seven tried mountaineers were out for more than two weeks, and this has been supplemented by all the visitors in the Park," reported Interior Secretary F. M. Goodwin on September 16 to Mrs. Whitehead. "There never has been a search in the national parks conducted with more vigor and effort than this one, and nothing has been left undone that could be humanly anticipated." Even a lion hunter from the US Biological Survey joined the search, bringing his dog to sniff the trails for the two men.

"The lakes and streams were thoroughly searched; all the trails in the rugged park were walked," noted authors Charles R. "Butch" Farabee Jr. and Stewart L. Udall in their book *Death, Daring & Disaster: Search and Rescue in the National Parks.* "With the coming snows, the search shifted to include a few criminal possibilities."

The relatively new head of the Federal Bureau of Investigation, J. Edgar Hoover, put his own resources to the test, following every lead and examining every shred of evidence that came to his G-men. Despite these efforts and the stack of detailed reports Hoover filed with the National Park Service, however, he soon ran out of options. There simply were no more leads to follow.

The Whitehead brothers were never found, and to this day no one knows what happened to them. Perhaps, like so many other unlucky visitors described in this book, they fell into McDonald Creek and were swept down into the murky depths of the lake. Perhaps their remains lay for eternity at the bottom of a steep cliff that the search parties—a meager group by today's standards—did not discover. Nearly one hundred years later, there is little hope that evidence will ever come to light to tell us what became of these young men.

MISSING FROM GOAT HAUNT

On July 17, 1934, Dr. F. H. Lumley, a professor of educational research at Ohio State University in Columbus, arrived at Glacier National Park with a railroad tour and decided that he'd had enough of the rails and was ready to spend some quality time in this magnificent park. He settled in at Many Glacier and made it his center of operation, taking many hikes through the park and making the most of his opportunities to enjoy the scenery and the brisk mountain air.

On August 13 he left Goat Haunt Campground, telling a guide that he planned to walk around Waterton Lake in Canada as part of a seventeen-mile hike on a tourist trail. Dr. Lumley planned to meet up later with a couple identified as Mr. and Mrs. R. D. Owen of Cambridge, Massachusetts, with whom he was supposed to reunite at a resort in Crossley Lake. But when the Owens checked into the resort later that day, Dr. Lumley had not arrived.

Days passed before hotel staff at Many Glacier contacted park officials to tell them that Dr. Lumley's baggage had remained at the hotel there since August 13, indicating that he had never called for the bags since he departed there on his way to Crossley Lake. Rangers finally made the connection between these bags and the calls they had received over the last several days from Lumley's family in Ohio, looking for a son who had not returned home to Ohio on schedule.

Park officials organized twenty-five "experienced woodsmen," who searched all the northern trails in the park, while other park employees checked all the hotels, chalets, and camps in the park to see if Dr. Lumley had simply changed his plans.

"Lumley said he was going to Waterton, Canada, and then out of the park," Owen told the Associated Press nearly two weeks later, on August 29, as the search intensified. He had not appeared at Waterton either, however, and investigators began making inquiries on August 30 of "all transportation agencies operating out of Waterton."

All this searching, however, turned up not a single lead. On September 4 Mrs. William McPherson of Columbus, a friend of the Lumley family, wrote a letter to Superintendent E. T. Scoyen at the park and suggested that Dr. Lumley was "greatly interested in climbing." She said that she and her husband had been in the park with Dr. Lumley during his stay at Many Glacier. "He went up Grinnell and Altyn mountains and hoped to climb others," she wrote. "He had climbed in the Bavarian Alps and in Rocky Mountain Park. He was a very fearless person. He may have tried one of the mountains near Goathaunt."

Park officials shifted the search to the park's mountain peaks in the area near Goat Haunt, focusing on Mount Cleveland—the park's highest mountain, where some members of a climbing party said that Lumley had mentioned an interest in scaling—but the effort continued to reveal no clues. As September came to a close and the Lumley family offered a five-hundred-dollar reward to anyone who could provide any ideas about where their son may have gone, park staff vowed to continue the search even though the park itself had closed for the winter.

Wintry weather with heavy snows finally brought the search to a close, with no trace of Dr. Lumley ever coming to light. To this day his disappearance remains a mystery.

WITH BARELY A TRACE

Patrick Terrence Whalen came from Cleveland, Ohio, but he was living in Portland, Oregon, when he decided to spend a couple of months in the fall of 2000 exploring Glacier National Park. At thirty-three, he was a registered nurse studying naturopathy, the field of natural health care, with the plan of becoming a doctor in the specialty. A seasoned hiker who had logged thousands of miles on the Pacific Crest Trail and hundreds of hours in national parks, Whalen seemed more than capable of finding his way around Glacier, even in the chilly-to-frigid weather of September, October, and November. Some accounts call him a "survivalist," but whether he himself would have defined his skills at that level, he certainly knew what he was about when making camp in the rugged Montana wilderness.

When his vehicle was found abandoned on November 2, 2000, at the Lake McDonald Lodge Restaurant—along US 89, at the eastern edge of the park near the Blackfeet reservation—there was no sign of Whalen. As far as anyone could tell, he had vanished into the Cut Bank Creek drainage, in the shadow of Bad Marriage Mountain and Medicine Grizzly Peak.

A park press release noted that his family had revealed some key information: Patrick Whalen had recently begun to exhibit some signs of mental illness. "Symptoms of unusual and potentially obsessive behavior, including paranoia," had become obvious to his family. They believed that these issues may have led him to do something uncharacteristic, like getting lost in Glacier's forests or taking unadvisable risks.

Winter was no time to search for a young man in the Montana wilderness, though attempts were made to locate him as soon as the park had established he was missing. The following May 27 a park ranger discovered an abandoned camp at the Atlantic Creek Backcountry Campground, along the North Fork of Cut Bank Creek. The items found at the campsite matched personal belongings Patrick would have had with him on a camping trip, according to his family. "Park officials do not believe Whalen wintered at the camp, but instead point to evidence suggesting the site had been abandoned since last fall," the *Missoulian* reported in August 2001.

Park rangers brought in a K-9 unit and performed a grid search of the area, searching for two days for any evidence that Whalen might have encountered foul play or had any kind of an accident. No other clues ever surfaced. In August 2001, the park reached out to the general public, asking for any information anyone had about where Whalen may have last been seen. He remains listed with the Glacier County Sheriff's Office as a missing person.

Eight years later, in 2008, his family held a memorial celebration of his life, bringing some kind of closure to an "incredibly long and painful" period of waiting, hoping, and resolving nothing at all.

FOREVER WANDERING

Compared to the case of Dr. F. H. Lumley, we know almost nothing of what happened to D. W. Cosby Bell, a man who set off to climb Mount Brown in July 1933 and never came down. Not a shred of media coverage gives us a glimpse into the manhunt, assuming there was one, and no further details ever came to light.

Likewise, the disappearance of twenty-one-year-old David Paul Wilson in 1963 provides us with a perplexing lack of information as well. A year after he started off to hike up Going-to-the-Sun Mountain, the Associated Press gives us only a tiny peek at what happened next. Wilson, who came to the park from his home in Severna Park, Maryland, decided to make the climb alone on August 2, 1963. When he did not return, rangers organized a search—one that continued informally a year later. "The park's chief ranger, Lyle McDowell, said every ranger who patrols the area, naturalists conducting hikes and park crews all watch for leads to the climber's fate, but nothing has been found," the *Independent Record* tells us on August 2, 1964.

The rangers did have a theory, however. "McDowell said officials think Wilson's body may be concealed in a glacial crevasse," the paper concluded.

Forty years would pass before another hiker ventured into the wilderness and vanished forever, this time with only a scant few additional clues. Sometime between May 29 and June 23, 2003, forty-year-old Larry Kimble of Dorr, Michigan, parked his dark blue 1998 GMC truck at the Rocky Point trailhead along the western shore of Lake McDonald. The Rocky Point Trail is a mile-long nature trail with a fairly small elevation change when compared with other popular trails in the park—a rise of about three hundred fifty feet over the course of the mile. The route crosses Fern Creek and continues to a loop with stunning views of Lake McDonald from Rocky Point, but much of the trail today crosses the land ravaged by the Robert Fire of July 2003. If you want to see what a massive forest fire does to a wooded landscape, this is the place to visit; you can also gain an understanding of the forest's ability to regenerate over time, as successional tree species including lodgepole pine, larch, ponderosa pine, and Douglas fir have already grown tall in this area, planted as their cones popped open in the flames and were fed by the nutrients in the remaining ash.

When Larry Kimble walked out into this forest, however, it was still old growth and lush with conifers and other northwestern trees. Somehow, on this easy trail, he met with a mishap that left no trace of struggle, no evidence of injury, and no sign of Kimble.

Weeks may have passed after this accident took place before anyone began to look for Kimble. On June 16 rangers noticed that Kimble's truck remained parked at the trailhead. They observed it day after day until they decided it was time for further investigation, and then impounded the truck on June 23. Inside they found an entrance admission receipt dated May 29.

Tracing the license plate, park officials called Kimble's relatives in Michigan to find out if they knew where he was. The family had reported Kimble as a missing person to their local police in Allegan County on June 20. With confirmation of the person for whom they were looking, rangers began an official search, placing flyers at the trailhead and distributing them throughout the park in hopes of finding someone who had spotted him. Kimble had not applied for a backcountry permit, nor was there any kind of camping equipment in the truck or any other kinds of supplies—in fact, his family assured rangers that he was not a camper. Searchers now had a photo, however, and they released a description of Kimble, citing his shoulder-length brown hair, brown eyes, height of six feet one inch, and weight of one hundred fifty to one hundred sixty pounds.

By June 27, when no sign of Kimble had turned up, rangers brought in teams of tracking dogs to help them search both on land and in the water. The dogs "indicated an interest" in the Lake McDonald area, but a July 3 search of Lake McDonald by divers of the Flathead County and North Valley Search and Rescue squads and the Flathead County Sheriff's Office—a total of eight divers and eight support people on the surface—produced no new clues.

"His family is very worried about him," Sergeant Tony Saucedo of the Allegan County Police Department told journalist Charlotte Weick at the *Penasee Globe* in Michigan on July 21. He said that Kimble's brother John told him that his brother "had not been seen since spring." Police searched his home, but found nothing to indicate any intention to disappear or to take his own life.

"Kimble is not known to be a hiker or camper and his travel itinerary was not known by family members," the *Globe* story continued. "Investigators could not find any record of recent lodging in or near the park."

Days later, with no new physical evidence, park officials and law enforcement refocused their investigation to try to determine if Kimble had any motivation to vanish. They determined that he had "recently split with his longtime girlfriend, but no one knows if that might have any relevance regarding his disappearance."

The Allegan police sent a detective to the girlfriend's home, but she had no new information to share. "She told Mathis that Kimble had expressed interest in visiting Glacier Park, but the ex-girlfriend said Kimble was not the type of outdoorsman who would head off into the backcountry alone," the *Missoula Independent* reported in mid-July.

Rangers conducted a second search with dogs on July 10 and planned a thorough grid search on July 11, but fire broke out on the east side of the park, and resources were reassigned to battle the blaze and control the flow of tourists around the area.

Two weeks later, on July 23, a lookout spotted the Robert Fire as it blazed up for ten acres along the North Fork of the Flathead River. In a matter of hours, it grew to 1,945 acres, with smoke visible from behind Apgar Mountain, and it began to move toward the Lake McDonald Valley. Three thousand people were evacuated from Lake McDonald while the fire began to look like it would head for West Glacier. In the ensuing days park management and fire crews lit a "back burn" fire to draw the fire northward, effectively protecting the town, but the Robert Fire continued to grow and the entire forest at Rocky Point burned to the ground—a tiny part of the 136,000 total acres consumed by the largest fire in Glacier's history.

If Larry Kimble's body remained somewhere in the forest, the fire turned it to ashes. The search ended, and the case will remain forever unsolved.

CHAPTER 14

Unclassified: Deaths by Unusual Causes

The story of Connie J. Lindsey's accident and its disastrous result receives the dubious honor of being "one of the most freakish in the history of Glacier Park," according to the Glacier Park Foundation's *Inside Trail* newsletter in the fall of 1998.

Lindsey, a forty-seven-year-old resident of Polson, Montana, had ridden a horse with her husband and two friends from Many Glacier to the Ptarmigan Tunnel, a pedestrian tunnel on a trail in a remote backcountry area. Lindsey was an experienced rider who often explored the backcountry trails on horseback with her husband, David. On this beautiful July 5, they would have encountered some snow along the trail, but nothing they would consider out of the ordinary or unusually challenging.

As rules and common sense recommended, all four riders dismounted and led their horses through the tunnel—a connecting route along a narrow ridge leading to the Belly River watershed—and then stopped to enjoy the scenery on the other side. Lindsey strolled about twenty-five yards from the tunnel gates, pausing at the waist-high stone parapet to admire the expansive view of the sheer cliffs and Elizabeth Lake below. Her horse stood beside her, nibbling at the snow on a nearby snowbank, while she took some pictures.

Suddenly the horse stumbled and jerked sideways, "perhaps reacting to the coldness of the snow," the newsletter suggests, in an attempt to apply some kind of logic to what happened next. "It knocked Lindsey onto the retaining wall, then lost its footing and fell on top of her. Horse and rider both rolled over the wall and fell for hundreds of feet."

Somehow recovering from the shock of seeing his wife fall, David rode five miles to Many Glacier for help. Rangers and rescue crews responded as quickly as they could with a helicopter and climbers, but they already knew that their mission would be one of recovery of the body rather than rescue. Climbers braved snow and scree-covered slopes to bring Connie Lindsey's body to the surface at about ten p.m., retrieving her from "a chimney in the rocks."

Understanding the Inexplicable

We can take every precaution, choose activities that appear to be quite safe, stay in familiar and popular areas of the park, and believe that we are minimizing our risks to life and limb . . . and still become the victim of that most inexplicable of hazards: the freak accident.

Some of these incidents, like the sad case of Connie Lindsey, spring from nothing more nefarious than bad luck. For example, while George McKinnon and Bert Ryan worked on repairs of the failing Two Medicine Bridge on September

16, 1914, under the supervision of contractor B. B. Gilliland, the damaged bridge suddenly collapsed. The falling debris broke Ryan's arm and fatally injured McKinnon. The *Report of the Secretary of the Interior* for that year noted that the men were making "necessary changes" to the bridge when it fell. Sadly for McKinnon, the changes probably should have been made years before.

Poor John Joe Pearce, a thirty-four-year-old National Park Service worker in 1933, took a tumble into the top of a rock crusher while he worked to oil the machine. He "either slipped or was blown below, where he was crushed between two large revolving wheels," the *Daily Inter Lake* reported. "He was found in the pit below the wheels with his neck broken and his left side crushed." Pearce received a burial with military honors through the local American Legion post.

A simple misstep along a road can mean certain death in Glacier, as Calgary, Alberta, resident Yvonne V. Waslovich discovered on August 31, 1986. She was walking along a mountain road in heavy fog, just off Going-to-the-Sun Road near Logan Pass, when she fell down a cliff, tumbling about one hundred fifty feet—a fall that would be virtually impossible to survive. A paramedic reached her while she was still alive, but her life ended about an hour later.

Donald Ash, a Whitefish resident in his late twenties, met his end on August 1, 1976, when he fell sixty feet from a spot on Going-to-the-Sun Road. He had stopped his car at Haystack Creek, four miles west of Logan Pass, to attempt to fill his canteen with creek water. Ash had only climbed down about ten feet when he lost his footing and tumbled down the rocky slope. He died at the scene.

In the case of David Olseth, riding a bicycle after dark on Going-to-the-Sun Road may have created an avoidable hazard, or it may have been something the thirty-year-old Whitefish man had done before—perhaps many times— with no mishaps. A moonlight ride on August 5, 2001, ended in disaster for the young man, however, when he gained too much speed on a downhill slope and lost control of his cycle. "He flipped over the rock wall along the Triple Arches section of the road and fell about 250 feet," the Associated Press reported two days later.

Olseth's parents, Dale and Nancy Olseth, managed to make something good happen in the face of this tragedy. In 2005 they made a gift of one hundred thousand dollars in David's name to build the Whitefish Skate Park, naming the park in their son's memory. The Dave Olseth Memorial Skatepark is located in Armory Park on East Second Street in Whitefish.

ADRENALINE RUSH

"If you can't make sacrifices for your dreams," carpenter-turned-base-jumper Beau Weiher told the website the Adrenalist in April 2013, "you should probably choose bigger dreams."

Weiher had given up his construction job in Durango, Colorado, shortly before the interview to move to Missoula, Montana, to devote himself entirely to the sport of BASE jumping. This high-adrenaline activity involves taking a flying leap from a fixed object, like a skyscraper, an antenna, a bridge, or a cliff (represented by the four letters in BASE as buildings, antennae, spans, and Earth), and breaking the fall by deploying a parachute at exactly the right moment.

BASE jumping is illegal in most national parks, including Glacier, but this does not necessarily stop passionate jumpers from attempting it within park boundaries. For a very brief time in 1980, the National Park Service allowed BASE jumpers to leap in Yosemite National Park with a permit. Jumpers found the park service's rules too restrictive, however, and began to disregard them—so much so that Yosemite returned to its ban on the sport just ten weeks after the first permit was issued.

In Glacier, BASE jumpers are very rare, park spokesperson Denise Germann told the *Missoulian* on September 17, 2014. "The last time we dealt with it was in the early 1990s," she said. "It's not a prevalent issue in the park."

Sadly, the media interview followed the last jump Beau Weiher would ever make. Weiher's body was discovered near Mount Siyeh on Sunday, September 14, with a deployed parachute spread out behind him. His family and friends told park dispatch that he had not returned from a day hike in the Piegan Pass and Mount Siyeh area on Saturday night, and rangers began a ground search on Sunday morning. By six p.m. that evening, helicopter personnel from Two Bear Air spotted the parachute on the ground below the mountain and directed search and rescue crews to the area, where they found Weiher's body.

GETTING THE SHOT

It's fitting that the last story I will tell in this book features a person who stepped past a boundary to take a photo.

In this case, Harold Addison of North Carolina decided he would capture a better image by risking his life and climbing over a retaining wall at a turnout about a mile east of Logan Pass. The seventy-four-year-old visitor lost his balance at the top of this cliff and fell forward, dropping between four hundred and five hundred feet before his fall ended on the rocks below.

The park dispatched a technical rescue team, sending one ranger rappelling down the cliff face to see if the mission would involve a rescue or retrieval of the body. After such a precipitous fall, Addison had died of massive trauma on impact. The rangers worked together to bring him up in a rescue litter on this mid-August day in 1999.

No doubt you expected to see many more such stories in this collection, but for the most part people who visit Glacier National Park understand the value of retaining walls, guardrails, and boundaries in keeping them safe on the park's many sheer cliffs. Perhaps it's the hairpin turns and narrow shoulders on Going-to-the-Sun Road that bring people to the very real conclusion that one bobbled step can be fatal, or maybe it's the intimidating glimpses of climbers in technical harnesses, ropes, and other gear scaling the faces of sedimentary peaks throughout the park—but whatever gives visitors to this park the clue that barriers are there for their safety, it's definitely working. Some parks have many sad tales to tell of people wading out to the middle of a rushing river just before it tumbles over a ledge and becomes a waterfall, or hopping from rock to rock at the top of a mountain to see a hair's-breadth additional viewscape from the top—and falling to their deaths. Glacier has very few of these entirely avoidable accidents in its records, a testament to its own efforts to warn tourists and keep them safe.

EPILOGUE: STAYING ALIVE IN THE NATIONAL PARKS

Are you ready to make the commitment to seeing all that is magnificent in Glacier National Park—its mountains, snowfields, forests, landscapes, wildflowers, animals, clear skies, lakes, and rivers—and living to tell the tale?

It's easier than you may think after reading this book, so let me remind you again: Fewer than three people per year actually die in the park, and some years no one dies at all. By following a few simple rules and taking some entirely reasonable precautions, you can make the most of your visit and come home with plenty of photos and accounts of your adventures.

Here are the basic guidelines you need, based on the advice of the National Park Service, Glacier park management, and experts in hiking and climbing safety.

AROUND THE PARK
- **Stay on designated trails.** Most people are not prepared to venture off-trail into the backcountry, and you can see plenty of marvelous sights from the established trails throughout the park. Note the directions you'll see on trail signs, and pay attention to blazes and markers to be sure you're still on your intended trail.

- **Stay behind protective fences, guardrails, and barriers.** Barriers are placed for your protection, *not* to keep you from enjoying the park. The moment you step beyond a guardrail or boundary, you risk injury.

- **Watch out for traffic.** When you stop at a pull-off along the side of a road, keep an eye out for oncoming traffic and fast-moving vehicles, just as you would on any busy street. Drivers gazing out over a spectacular view may not see you on the road, so watch out for people who are not watching out for you.

- **If you're driving, watch the road.** It's easy to be distracted by everything there is to see at Glacier, so if you want more time to enjoy a view, pull over into an area designated for that purpose and stop. Pedestrians, bicyclists, and people on horseback are everywhere along the park's major roadways—so keep an eye out.

- **Enjoy wildlife from a safe distance.** Mountain goats, bighorn sheep, bears, and elk all can feel threatened when humans get too close. Many of these animals will charge or attack you if you try to get in close for a photo. To get great photos, shoot with a telephoto lens from a safe distance away. If you're in your car and you spot wildlife from the road, pull over at the first available area and take your photos from inside your car. Above all, do not feed any wildlife in the park.

Hiking—Frontcountry or Backcountry

- **Don't hike alone.** The lure of solitude in the wild may be very attractive, but take note of the number of lone hikers described in this book who went missing for weeks, months, or even indefinitely. Hiking and camping with at least one other person can make the difference between a great day on the trail and a misadventure that ends in tragedy.

- **File your plan with a ranger.** If you're planning a lengthy wilderness hike or climb, you will need a backcountry permit to camp—which means that you will file a hiking plan at a ranger station or visitor center. Even if you don't plan to camp, it's a good idea to let rangers know where you intend to go and when you plan to return. With a million acres of land to search, the plan you file will allow rangers to narrow the field quickly if they need to locate you in a crisis.

- **Listen to rangers.** People who work in the park daily know which trails may be compromised by weather events, where avalanches and rockslides may be possible, where forest fires are burning within the park, and whether it's advisable to attempt the hike or climb you have in mind. If they warn you not to take a certain route, think very seriously about changing your plans.

- **Sign the trail register.** It may seem like a folksy tradition, but your signature in the trail register can save your life. It helps rangers discover exactly where you started your hike, so they can narrow a search if you become lost in the wilderness. Hikers who took the same trail in the last few days also may make note of unusual obstacles like rockslides, washed-out stream crossings, icy areas, or bears in the vicinity. Take heed of these warnings as you plan your route.

- **Carry more than you need.** Survival can become critical in the wilderness, so at the very least bring extra food, clothing, ways to keep warm, and a way to signal your location. Many hiking associations have their own list of the Ten Essentials you should bring on any hike, but here is the most widely accepted classic list:

  - Map
  - Compass (or other navigation tool, like a GPS)
  - Sunglasses and sunscreen
  - Extra clothing, including rain gear
  - Headlamp or flashlight
  - First-aid supplies
  - Fire starter—material that will ignite quickly and burn long enough for you to get a fire started
  - Matches
  - Knife
  - Extra food and water

- In addition, many hiking clubs recommend that you bring emergency shelter, a repair kit and tools (including a roll of duct tape), and a water filter kit when you hike in Glacier. If you need to signal your location, a mirror can be invaluable.

- **Know your limits.** Many hikers and climbers come to Glacier to take on a greater challenge than they have ever tried before. If you're one of these adventurers, be sure that you understand the kinds of skills required to complete the climb successfully. Hike or climb with someone who has the requisite experience to be sure your party gets home safely, and take all the necessary precautions, from carrying the right gear to recognizing that the challenge may be too great.

- **Watch your step on snowfields.** Even if you're not planning a technical climb across a glacier or snowfield, you may be fascinated by the opportunity to walk in snow in July. These snow-covered areas are not like your backyard, however: Snow can hide large crevasses in the ice below, and a wrong step can send you plunging down several stories into a very cold place. Think twice before walking out onto open snow.

- **Watch out for loose scree and shale.** Glacier is not a granite park, not even near the Granite Park Chalet (the igneous rock there is basalt). These mountains are made of sedimentary rock, so ledges and slopes can be as flaky as piecrust and give way under your feet. Step carefully and gauge the stability of a surface before you tread there, especially if you're walking along narrow ledges. Many climbing and hiking accidents result from unstable rock underfoot.

- **Check for avalanche advisories.** Call the Flathead Avalanche Center at (406) 257-8402 for updates about the potential for avalanches in specific areas of the park.

ON AND AROUND WATER

In Glacier National Park and in many other large wilderness parks throughout the National Park Service system, drowning is the number-one cause of death. Take some basic precautions to enjoy Glacier's extensive system of lakes, rivers, and streams without incident.

- **Understand that this water is very, very cold.** Fueled mostly by glacial meltwater and snowmelt, these waterways usually hover at just above the freezing point. A fall into water this cold can produce hypothermia, the condition that leads to freezing to death. Your best bet is to stay out of this water and enjoy it from the safety of the shore—or from a boat.

- **Stay off of slippery or moss-covered rocks and logs.** It may look like fun to hop from one boulder to the next in the middle of a rushing stream, but you will be surprised at how slick these rocks become when they're wet. Many deaths result from people slipping and falling from these rocks into frigid water.

- **Don't wade in or ford swift streams.** The water is moving faster than you think, and it's deeper and colder than you realize. You can be swept away by the current, and the cold will take over very quickly once you're in the water.

- **Don't wade into a stream at the top of a waterfall.** It's hard to believe that this needs to be said, but people die in Glacier and other parks (most famously Yosemite) because they wade out into a rushing stream to get a photo of a waterfall from the top. Here's a lifesaving tip from my husband and me, the author and photographer of the book *Hiking Waterfalls in New York*: There's nothing to see up there at the top of the falls. You'll get a much better photo from the bottom—and from the shore.

- **If you fly fish, choose a fairly calm stream.** It's no fun to fish if you're struggling against the current all morning, and it's less fun if the current wins. Talk to a ranger about the best and safest places to fish in the park on the day of your visit.

- **Stay in your boat.** Keep your hands and arms in the boat, and don't stand up or lean over the side. Boats can capsize, and Glacier's lakes can be hundreds of feet deep.

- **Wear a life jacket.** If your boat does capsize, your best chance for survival is to stay at the surface, where you can be found and retrieved quickly. At Glacier none of the people who drowned when their boats capsized were wearing life jackets. Learn from their example.

- **Carry water filtration equipment.** If you are camping in the backcountry, you will need an approved filter if you plan to draw on the park's waterways. The parasite *Giardia lamblia* is found in the park's water; it causes giardiasis, a disease that gives you cramps, persistent diarrhea, and nausea. Your best defense against this is to carry water from one of the park's treated water systems.

About Bears

Both black bears and grizzly bears live in Glacier, and hikers and campers often encounter them. If you follow these guidelines for visitor safety, you will enjoy your bear sighting from a safe distance.

- **Make noise when hiking.** For all their size and power, bears have only average hearing and rather poor eyesight. Make plenty of noise when you're hiking—talk, sing, call out, and clap your hands at regular intervals. Bear bells generally are not loud enough to let the animals know you're on your way. Once the bear hears you coming, chances are good that it will move away from the trail and leave you alone.

- **Assume the bears are nearby.** Even the most popular and well-used trails may go through bear country, so don't assume that there are no bears there because so many people hike here daily. Keep making noise (and ignore the people who give you the evil eye for being noisy), and keep your eyes open for bears in the area.

- **Watch out for surprises.** When you approach streams, shrubs full of berries, fields of cow parsnip or glacier lilies, or areas of dense vegetation, keep your eyes open for bears. As they can't always smell or hear you, you may startle a bear by approaching fairly quietly.

- **Do not approach bears.** Bears are not tame, and they are not zoo animals. You have come to their natural habitat in the wild, so you want to steer clear of them as much as possible. Don't try to get closer for a better photo. While deaths from bear attacks have been scant throughout the park's history, visitors have been mauled and sustained serious injuries because they tried to get too close. Says the park's website: "Never intentionally get close to a bear. Individual bears have their own personal space requirements, which vary depending on their mood. Each will react differently and its behavior can't be predicted. All bears are dangerous and should be respected equally."

- **Carry bear spray.** Pepper spray is one good defense against a charging bear. Nontoxic with no permanent effect, it triggers "temporary incapacitating discomfort" in the bear, which can halt an attack and give you the opportunity to get away from the bear. If a bear charges you, aim the aerosol directly in the bear's face. This is not a bear repellent—spraying it on yourself (as you would an insect repellent) will not keep bears away. As the park's guidelines note, "Under no circumstances should bear spray create a false sense of security or serve as a substitute for standard safety precautions in bear country."

- **If you encounter a bear, do this.** As every bear will react differently to you, there is no set protocol that will result in a surefire escape. Here are the guidelines offered by Glacier National Park (for more bear tips visit www.nps.gov/glac/planyourvisit/bears.htm):

- Talk quietly or not at all; the time to make loud noise is before you encounter a bear.

- Try to detour around the bear if possible.

- Do not run! Back away slowly, but stop if it seems to agitate the bear.

- Try to assume a nonthreatening posture. Turn sideways, or bend at the knees to appear smaller.

- Use peripheral vision. Bears may interpret direct eye contact as threatening.

- Drop something (not food) to distract the bear. Keep your pack on for protection in case of an attack.

- If a bear attacks and you have pepper spray, use it!

- If the bear makes contact, protect your chest and abdomen by falling to the ground on your stomach, or assuming a fetal position to reduce the severity of an attack. Cover the back of your neck with your hands. Do not move until you are certain the bear has left.

- **Store food safely.** When bears find human food in campsites, they learn to come back to these campsites again and again to devour table scraps or plunder trash cans. As we saw in the story of the Night of the

Grizzlies in 1967 (see chapter 6), these bears can lose their aversion to humans and begin to see us as prey. As you plan your backcountry trip, check with the park to find out the latest requirements for food storage—and at the very least, store your food in the bear-proof lockers and/or poles you will find at all sixty-three backcountry campsites throughout the park.

Follow these guidelines to make your visit to Glacier National Park the experience of a lifetime you hope it will be. Once again, I urge you to join more than two million people who discover and explore this park every year, with the knowledge that a few simple precautions will help you make certain that your trip is memorable for all the right reasons: the outdoor adventures, the wildlife sightings, the spectacular landscapes, and the people you encounter here at the Crown of the Continent.

APPENDIX: LIST OF DEATHS 1913–2015

Deaths in Glacier National Park 1913–2015 (in order of date)

NAME	AGE	DATE OF DEATH	CAUSE	LOCATION
Prince, Joe		1/8/1913	Exposure	Cut Bank
Fletcher, Dr. Calvin		8/13/1913	Fell while hiking	Blackfoot Glacier
McKinnon, George		9/16/1914	Bridge collapse	Two Medicine
White, George		7/22/1915	Intoxication	Many Glacier
Davis, Jane	39	6/25/1916	Drowning	Two Medicine River
Kettlesand, J. D.		9/1/1919	Hiking accident	St. Mary Lake
Unknown bus driver		9/8/1922	Vehicle accident	Divide Hill
Jones, Samantha	18	7/1/1923	Drowning	Lake McDonald
Huber, Fred W., Jr.	19	7/1/1923	Drowning	Lake McDonald
Peterson, Ester	20	6/29/1924	Fell while hiking	Altyn Peak
Fly, Donald T.		7/4/1924	Drowning	St. Mary Lake
Whitehead, Joseph	29	8/24/1924	Missing, presumed dead	Between Granite Lake and Lake McDonald
Whitehead, William A.	22	8/24/1924	Missing, presumed dead	Between Granite Lake and Lake McDonald
Unidentified man		1925	Drowning	Lake McDonald
Unidentified hunter		1925	Drowning	St. Mary Falls
Longini, Lena	19	7/15/1925	Drowning	St. Mary Falls
Longini, Harry	11	7/15/1925	Drowning	St. Mary Falls
Wheeler, J. B.		8/14/1925	Exposure	Lake Ellen Wilson
Wheeler, Mrs. J. B.		8/14/1925	Exposure	Lake Ellen Wilson
Rudbergin, Charles		1926	Construction accident	Going-to-the-Sun Road
McAfee, William B.		2/9/1926	Suicide	Kishenehn Ranger Station
Helander, Ole	37	2/7/1927	Exposure	Lake McDonald
Clark, Stanley	33	6/27/1931	Drowning	St. Mary Lake
Rosenquist, Carl		8/26/1931	Falling object	Going-to-the-Sun Road
Swanson, Gust	48	7/14/1932	Falling object	1.5 miles east of Logan Pass
Bell, D. W. Cosby		1933	Missing, presumed dead	Mount Brown

List of Deaths 1913–2015

NAME	AGE	DATE OF DEATH	CAUSE	LOCATION
Pearce, John Joe	34	11/27/1933	Construction accident	16 miles north of Glacier Park
Faber, Rt. Rev. William F.	74	7/20/1934	Exposure	Two Medicine
Greppo, M., Jr.	18 (?)	7/23/1934	Drowning	Sherburne Lake
Montemarano, A.	18 (?)	7/23/1934	Drowning	Sherburne Lake
Cooper, Gilbert	18 (?)	7/23/1934	Drowning	Sherburne Lake
Lumley, Dr. F. H.	27	8/13/1934	Missing, presumed dead	Goat Haunt
Kelley, Frank	60s	1/14/1935	Pneumonia	Lake McDonald
Kelley, Mrs. Frank	60s	1/14/1935	Pneumonia	Lake McDonald
Hayden, Dudley, Jr.	2	3/21/1935	Drowning	Lubec
Bogar, Geraldine	15	7/7/1935	Vehicle accident	North Fork Road
Gray, Herbert	16	7/26/1936	Climbing accident	Garden Wall
Oastler, Dr. Frank	65	8/2/1936	Heart attack	Many Glacier
Campbell, Lloyd	34	8/24/1937	Vehicle accident	Going-to-the-Sun Road
Shepard, Gilbert	19	6/20/1938	Climbing accident	Grinnell Point
Aldrich, Andrew J.	20	1/6/1939	Falling object	Apgar Flats
Owens, Arrah	69	7/15/1940	Natural causes	Josephine Lake
Kippen, N. A.		8/20/1940	Hiking accident	Many Glacier
Olson, Mrs. Simon	48	6/3/1941	Drowning	Many Glacier
Sibley, Cal Garver	23	12/27/1941	Burned to death	Apgar
Fehlberg, Eunice	40	7/5/1942	Drowning	Kintla Lake
Lee, Major Fred P.	48	10/12/1949	Drowning	McDonald Creek
Stokes, Robert	18	7/12/1950	Climbing accident	Mount Wilbur
Denney, Frank A.		7/27/1950	Drowning	St. Mary Lake
Pinney, James B.	30s	9/13/1950	Drowning	Kintla Lake
Provine, John C.	30s	9/13/1950	Drowning	Kintla Lake
Olinger, Aubrey	30s	9/13/1950	Drowning	Kintla Lake
Unidentified flag man		1950 or 1951	Fell while hiking	Going-to-the-Sun Road
Thomas, J. Louis		7/10/1951	Drowning	Two Medicine Lake
Norris, Charles	19	7/28/1951	Vehicle accident	St. Mary Bridge
Byrd, Bernida M.	8 months	8/5/1951	Falling object	Near Avalanche Campground

NAME	AGE	DATE OF DEATH	CAUSE	LOCATION
Dion, Robert	17	7/29/1952	Climbing accident	Little Chief Mountain
Stewart, Frank B.	74	8/3/1952	Drowning	St. Mary River
Beaton, George H.	45	5/26/1953	Avalanche	Going-to-the-Sun Road
Whitford, William A.	45	5/26/1953	Avalanche	Going-to-the-Sun Road
Kasen, Peter Allen	18	8/6/1953	Climbing accident	Mount Helen
Kays, Pat	18	6/30/1954	Drowning	Sherburne Lake
Larson, James	18	8/8/1954	Drowning	Swiftcurrent Lake
Showen, Albert L.	64	2/15/1955	Hiking accident	Park headquarters
Washburn, John		2/28/1955	Natural causes	Apgar at residence
Johnson, June B.	20	7/21/1955	Climbing accident	Altyn Peak
Jam, John S.	26	8/21/1955	Vehicle accident	Many Glacier
McMullin, George	51	4/10/1956	Hiking accident	Park headquarters
Mathison, Ken	47	7/15/1956	Fell while hiking	Going-to-the-Sun Road
Meuser, William L.	69	7/21/1956	Natural causes	Going-to-the-Sun Road
Miller, L. E.	62	7/27/1956	Hiking accident	Swiftcurrent Pass
Seargent, Victor E.	60	7/10/1958	Heart attack	On a road (driving)
Jensen, Mrs. Jean	23	8/16/1958	Natural causes	Lake McDonald Lodge
Bowman, Leo		5/31/1959	Vehicle accident	Many Glacier
Carmack, John		6/21/1959	Hiking accident	Park headquarters
Lynch, Robert D.	33	7/23/1959	Vehicle accident	US 2
Grist, James D.	52	7/23/1959	Vehicle accident	US 2
Stone, Michael	13	7/26/1960	Drowning	Upper McDonald Creek
Steinmetz, Frederick R.	18	7/28/1960	Fell while hiking	Red Gap Pass
Mayall, Lillian	52	8/28/1960	Fell while hiking	McDonald Falls
Moylan, James F.	17	6/21/1961	Climbing accident	Mount Henkel
Evans, B. H.	72	7/29/1961	Hiking accident	Going-to-the-Sun Road
Scott, Gordon E.	43	8/7/1961	Heart attack	St. Mary Campground
Dickman, Elberta	42	6/28/1962	Drowning	Upper McDonald Creek
Leckie, Alice Jean	52	6/28/1962	Falling object	Garden Wall
Larson, Ronald W.	23	9/2/1962	Vehicle accident	Sprague Creek Campground
Culp, Harry		9/7/1962	Natural causes	Many Glacier Hotel

NAME	AGE	DATE OF DEATH	CAUSE	LOCATION
Delaney, Jerome T.	19	6/18/1963	Climbing accident	Mount Pollock
Trenor, Gregory W. A.	6	6/26/1963	Drowning	Upper McDonald Creek
Dumay, Thomas	21	6/28/1963	Drowning	Upper Lake McDonald
Wilson, David Paul	21	8/2/1963	Missing, presumed dead	Going-to-the-Sun Mountain
McPhillips, Frank	70	8/23/1963	Drowning	Two Medicine Lake
Gerrish, Paul J.	5	7/16/1964	Vehicle accident	Park headquarters
Fulton, Clara	64	7/21/1964	Natural causes	Lake Josephine
Gelston, Kenneth	22	7/25/1964	Fell while hiking	St. Mary Falls
Jones, Paul E.	46	5/11/1965	Suicide	Near Avalanche Campground
Davie, Christine	8 months	7/20/1965	Natural causes	McDonald Lodge
Noldon, Henry M.	65	7/25/1965	Hiking accident	Lake McDonald
VanMun, Laura Jean	6	8/4/1965	Fell while hiking	Trick Falls
Smith, C. K. B.	77	8/12/1965	Hiking accident	Two Medicine
Ley, Audrey	56	8/19/1965	Hiking accident	Many Glacier
Flammond, Everett	20	6/14/1966	Vehicle accident	Many Glacier Road
Kittson, James	16	6/14/1966	Vehicle accident	Many Glacier Road
Devaney, Rev. Joseph H.	52	7/30/1966	Fell while hiking	Mount Oberlin
Schreiber, Rev. Paul F.	38	8/13/1966	Fell while hiking	Logan Pass cliff
Jungster, Hans	49	3/7/1967	Hiking accident	Apgar
Tettlebach, Douglas	20	7/3/1967	Climbing accident	Mount Custer
Helgeson, Julie M.	19	8/13/1967	Bear attack	Granite Park Campground
Koons, Michele L.	19	8/13/1967	Bear attack	Trout Lake Campground
Moors, Keith	33	12/28/1967	Falling object	Nyack–Walton
Jones, Larry	29	5/26/1968	Suicide	Apgar picnic area
Neale, Diane	19	6/22/1968	Vehicle accident	Many Glacier Road
Gettys, Paul	17	7/24/1969	Climbing accident	Altyn Peak
Long, Rodney W.	50	8/23/1969	Heart attack	Fish Creek Campground
Kanzler, Jerry	18	12/30/1969	Avalanche	Mount Cleveland
Progreba, Clare	22	12/30/1969	Avalanche	Mount Cleveland
Levitan, Mark	20	12/30/1969	Avalanche	Mount Cleveland

NAME	AGE	DATE OF DEATH	CAUSE	LOCATION
Martin, Ray	22	12/30/1969	Avalanche	Mount Cleveland
Anderson, James	18	12/30/1969	Avalanche	Mount Cleveland
Mellett, Melvin M.	63	5/19/1970	Hiking accident	Eddie's Cap, Apgar
Delaney, George		6/1/1970	Drowning	Lower St. Mary Lake
Delaney, Herb		6/1/1970	Drowning	Lower St. Mary Lake
Personett, Robert	23	6/29/1970	Drowning	North Fork River
Fisher, Neil T.	9	7/5/1970	Drowning	Lower McDonald Creek
Straley, Chris B.	56	7/22/1970	Hiking accident	Many Glacier Hotel
Perry, Roscoe M.	72	12/11/1970	Vehicle accident	US 2, Goat Lick Area
Mattson, Lowell	40	2/6/1971	Vehicle accident	North Fork River
Kitzman, Maynard E.	55	7/4/1971	Vehicle accident	Many Glacier
Pokorney, Francis	59	7/5/1971	Hiking accident	Many Glacier Hotel
Boughner, Sally	22	7/30/1971	Drowning	Upper McDonald Creek
Matthews, Ronald	32	8/15/1971	Fell while hiking	Sperry Glacier
North, Perihan	43	7/5/1972	Drowning	St. Mary Lake
Grove, Nathan	64	8/24/1972	Hiking accident	Grinnell Glacier Trail
Sander, Adrian	62	8/6/1973	Hiking accident	St. Mary Campground
Staner, Karl J.	72	8/21/1973	Fell while hiking	McDonald Falls
Dunn, Michael	22	8/23/1973	Drowning	Upper Two Medicine Lake
Chrissman, Roy	18	7/6/1974	Vehicle accident	US 2, west of Goat Lick
Neyer, Michael	22	7/15/1974	Climbing accident	Rising Wolf Mountain
Hunting, John P.	19	8/18/1974	Climbing accident	Stoney Indian Peak
Finley, Gregory A.	19	7/4/1975	Climbing accident	Mount Brown
Donovan, Donald	45	11/1/1975	Airplane crash	Two Medicine area
See, Kathryn M.	31	11/1/1975	Airplane crash	Two Medicine area
Krell, James	42	6/18/1976	Drowning	Lake McDonald
Raider, Sam	27	7/3/1976	Climbing accident	Mount Clements
Boos, David	17	7/15/1976	Climbing accident	Mount Siyeh
Ash, Donald William	29	8/1/1976	Hiking accident	Haystack Butte
Mahoney, Mary Pat	21	9/23/1976	Bear attack	Many Glacier Campground
Barry, David Noel	20	6/23/1977	Drowning	Wilbur Creek

NAME	AGE	DATE OF DEATH	CAUSE	LOCATION
Hill, Randy	22	6/23/1977	Drowning	Wilbur Creek
Squibb, Margaret W.	18	7/2/1978	Climbing accident	Rising Wolf Mountain
Brown, Nancy Anderson	24	7/31/1978	Fell while hiking	Grinnell Point
D'Arcy, Doug	17	6/13/1979	Drowning	St. Mary Lake
Berger, Troy	17	6/13/1979	Drowning	St. Mary Lake
Griggs, Coleen G.	20	8/31/1979	Vehicle accident	St. Mary
Ammerman, Jane A.	19	7/24/1980	Bear attack	St. Mary
Eberly, Kim	19	7/24/1980	Bear attack	St. Mary
Gordon, Laurence	33	9/30/1980	Bear attack	Elizabeth Lake
Ellis, David H.	69	6/17/1981	Hiking accident	Many Glacier
McLean, Carla	26	7/12/1981	Vehicle accident	Two Medicine
Dolack, Kevin P.	7	7/22/1981	Drowning	Upper McDonald Creek
Danielowski, Betty	40	7/27/1981	Drowning	Upper McDonald Creek
Danielowski, Don	41	7/27/1981	Drowning	Upper McDonald Creek
Bareham, Charles	30	8/22/1981	Fell while hiking	Hidden Lake Trail
Donaghey, H. J.	23	8/29/1981	Climbing accident	Mount Stimson
Oaks, DeVali	12	6/15/1982	Drowning	Avalanche Creek
Lieser, Walter E.	84	8/24/1982	Hiking accident	Many Glacier Hotel
Handford, Lisa	20	5/28/1983	Drowning	Haystack Butte Creek
Hatley, Teddy	20	5/28/1983	Drowning	Lower Kintla Lake
Pongrace, Frederick H.	31	7/13/1983	Homicide	1 mile above Loop
Sullivan, Paul	48	7/21/1983	Hiking accident	Village Inn
Fernekes, Steven	27	10/12/1983	Climbing accident	South Swiftcurrent Glacier
Herron, Robert W.	34	1/24/1984	Vehicle accident	US 2, east of Walton Ranger Station
Tolley, Mary E.	72	8/30/1984	Hiking accident	Bowman Lake Campground
Tangvold, Thor	19	6/10/1985	Climbing accident	Ptarmigan Falls
Walton, Robert S.		9/4/1985	Vehicle accident	St. Mary entrance station
Conway, James	28	9/5/1985	Airplane crash	Near Siyeh Bend
Conway, Judith	57	9/5/1985	Airplane crash	Near Siyeh Bend

NAME	AGE	DATE OF DEATH	CAUSE	LOCATION
Frahn, Gerald	68	9/5/1985	Hiking accident	Apgar Campground
Soderlund, Peter	25	4/29/1986	Suicide	Near Packers Roost
Bauer, Charles	27	5/31/1986	Fell while hiking	Reynolds Mountain
McCauley, James	80	7/5/1986	Hiking accident	Near Avalanche Campground
Reed, Ross	43	8/3/1986	Vehicle accident	Weeping Wall
Jacobsen, Geraldine	64	8/7/1986	Fell from horse	Upper Lake McDonald Road
Waslovich, Yvonne V.	34	8/31/1986	Fell while taking photo	East of Logan Pass
Gibbs, Charles	40	4/25/1987	Bear attack	Walton Subdistrict
Cox, Bradley J.	32	6/4/1987	Vehicle accident	Going-to-the-Sun Road near Triple Arches
Goeden, Gary	29	7/1987	Bear attack	Appekuny Cirque
Hall, Robert	34	9/1/1987	Vehicle accident	Many Glacier Road
Isch, Harry	69	7/21/1988	Heart attack	Near Hidden Lake, on trail
Schustrom, Barbara	50	4/2/1990	Drowning	Near Upper McDonald Creek
Skeen, Thomas E.	81	6/25/1990	Hiking accident	Apgar
Grapatin, Dale	45	7/16/1990	Climbing accident	Chief Mountain
Wiebe, Norman J.	29	8/8/1990	Vehicle accident	Going-to-the-Sun Road near Triple Arches
McCartie, Brian	21	9/8/1990	Climbing accident	Bishop's Cap
Fetter, Edgar M.	22	3/1991	Vehicle accident	Going-to-the-Sun Road east of East Side Tunnel
Ochenrieder, Gordon	45	8/15/1991	Climbing accident	Southern slope of Mount Siyeh
Lecke, Sandra	46	8/17/1991	Hiking accident	Near Logan Creek
Smith, Willard A.	57	2/12/1992	Airplane crash	Near Logan Pass
Smith, Marion V.	54	2/12/1992	Airplane crash	Near Logan Pass
Hodges, Merwin	79	5/19/1992	Hiking accident	Two Medicine Lake
Efraimson, George	63	7/11/1992	Hiking accident	Kelly's Camp Visitor
Skibsrud, Josh	20	7/19/1992	Climbing accident	Mount Gould
Petranyi, John	40	10/3/1992	Bear attack	Trail to Granite Park
Wood, Suzanne R.	52	6/18/1993	Hiking accident	Many Glacier Campground
Dexort, Sophia	79	6/20/1993	Vehicle accident	US 2, Walton area
Nixon, Francine A.	48	7/24/1993	Drowning	Upper McDonald Creek

NAME	AGE	DATE OF DEATH	CAUSE	LOCATION
Breitbart, Lela	24	6/21/1995	Avalanche	Trail southeast of Avalanche Lake
Schubert, Taggart	25	1/12/1996	Climbing accident	Jackson Glacier
Swanson, Margaret	78	6/14/1996	Vehicle accident	On Going-to-the-Sun Road near Wilson
Kamochi, Tsuyoshi	30	6/23/1996	Falling object	Rimrock, Going-to-the-Sun Road
Jercinovic, Toma	22	7/28/1996	Climbing accident	Above Avalanche Lake
Robison, Mark	24	7/3/1997	Climbing accident	On Rainbow Glacier
Foster, Chris	24	7/3/1997	Climbing accident	On Rainbow Glacier
Truszkowski, Matt	25	7/6/1997	Climbing accident	Mount Sinopah, Two Medicine
Dokken, Roger	62	9/1/1997	Climbing accident	On Mount Cleveland
Dahl, Craig	26	5/17/1998	Bear attack	Appistoki Falls
Lindsey, Connie J.	47	7/5/1998	Riding accident	Ptarmigan Tunnel
Donald-Nelson, Brian	27	7/15/1998	Fell while hiking	Red Gap Pass
Simpson, William		8/4/1998	Hiking accident	Rising Sun
Ryan, Craig	56	7/21/1999	Climbing accident	Mount Clements
Addison, Harold	74	8/13/1999	Fell while taking photo	Going-to-the-Sun Road
Laird, Dale	42	4/16/2000	Airplane crash	Kennedy Lake/Mount Henkel
Mayer, Henry	59	7/24/2000	Heart attack	Going-to-the-Sun Road (bicycling)
Wolk, Christopher B.	26	8/9/2000	Falling object	Swiftcurrent Creek
Whalen, Patrick T.	33	11/2/2000	Missing, presumed dead	Atlantic Creek Backcountry Campground
Parks, James M.	83	6/11/2001	Natural causes	Lake McDonald Lodge
Harris, Don Fogg	85	6/14/2001	Fell while hiking	Going-to-the-Sun Road
Olseth, David	30	8/5/2001	Bicycle accident	Going-to-the-Sun Road
Krajewski, Wojciech	22	8/13/2001	Climbing accident	Mount Jackson
Nery, Manita Felicidad Diaz	59	6/28/2002	Drowning	Avalanche Creek
Hart, Thomas	17	7/23/2002	Drowning	Hudson Bay Creek
Wiesike, Matthew Colin	20	8/5/2002	Fell while hiking	Reynolds Mountain

NAME	AGE	DATE OF DEATH	CAUSE	LOCATION
Smith, Manville J.	61	9/5/2002	Hiking accident	Near Sperry Chalet
Kimble, Larry	40	6/27/2003	Missing, presumed dead	Lake McDonald area
Peckham, Richard	73	8/15/2003	Natural causes	Near Siyeh Pass
Horter, Mark	49	7/8/2004	Hiking accident	3 miles up Scenic Point Trail–Two Medicine
Cohn, Howard	46	7/27/2004	Exposure	Grinnell Glacier
Makescoldweather, Angel Star	19	9/3/2004	Vehicle accident	Going-to-the-Sun Road Granite Creek Area
Johnston, David	64	7/20/2005	Hiking accident	Upper Grinnell Lake
Brooks, Dennis	43	11/21/2005	Drowning	Upper McDonald Creek
Grecco, Ronald	66	6/19/2008	Hiking accident	Iceberg/Ptarmigan Trail
Hwa, Yi-Jien	27	8/8/2008	Fell while hiking	Chute above Avalanche Lake
Colburn, Bruce	53	10/24/2008	Suicide	Kintla Lake drainage
Greene, James R.	22	7/14/2009	Drowning	Swiftcurrent Lake
Labunetz, William	67	8/22/2009	Fell while hiking	Ahearn Mountain
Zlatnik, George S.	51	9/9/2009	Vehicle accident	Going-to-the-Sun Road
Wright, Brian C.	37	3/31/2010	Avalanche	Mount Shields
McNamara, Elizabeth G.	62	6/18/2010	Drowning	Virginia Falls
Croff, Clinton	30	7/29/2010	Suicide	Two Medicine Road
Trisdale, Charles	81	8/12/2010	Hiking accident	Logan Pass parking lot
Sloan, Michael	30	9/21/2010	Drowning	Lake McDonald at McDonald Creek
Friesen, Ladell	34	2/22/2011	Vehicle accident	US 2, mile marker 182
Ryan, Nicholas	30	7/18/2011	Fell while hiking	Grinnell Glacier Trail
Fish, Richard	70	7/23/2011	Vehicle accident	Going-to-the-Sun Road near Logan Creek
Fergason, David	69	8/23/2011	Hiking accident	Gunsight Pass Trail
Rigby, Jacob "Jake"	27	8/29/2011	Climbing accident	Peak 8888, between Park and Ole Creeks
Kreiser, Jakson	19	7/29/2012	Drowning	Above head of Hidden Lake
Blair, Merrill	69	8/20/2012	Natural causes	Rising Sun Restaurant

List of Deaths 1913–2015

NAME	AGE	DATE OF DEATH	CAUSE	LOCATION
Hughes, David	67	9/25/2012	Drowning	North Fork of the Flathead River
Reddig, Amy	28	3/13/2013	Drowning	Lake McDonald Lodge area
Huseman, Charles	64	6/26/2013	Fell while hiking	Rimrock on Highline Trail
Johnson, Cody	25	7/7/2013	Homicide	Cliff next to the Loop
Flores, Cesar	21	7/9/2013	Climbing accident	Apikuni Ridge
Needham, Matthew	21	7/25/2013	Climbing accident	Grinnell Point
Sylvester, Abigail	33	7/13/2014	Drowning	McDonald Creek
Weiher, Beau	22	9/14/2014	BASE jumping	Mount Siyeh
Avalos, Brandon Luis	18	9/18/2014	Fell while hiking	Big Drift area
Unidentified man (name never released)		3/25/2015	Suicide	Going-to-the-Sun Road

INDEX

ABOUT THE AUTHOR

Randi Minetor is the author of more than thirty-five books, including the Passport to Your National Parks Companion *Guides* series and books about individual parks, battlefields, and historic sites throughout the National Park Service system. She has visited more than 300 of America's 408 national parks in forty-seven states. Her titles include National Park Pocket Guides on Great Smoky Mountains, Acadia, Zion, Bryce Canyon, and Everglades National Parks and Gulf Islands National Seashore, and Historical Tours series books including Gettysburg National Battlefield Park, Fredericksburg National Battlefield, Washington, DC, the New York Immigrant Experience, and New Orleans. She is also the author of the upcoming *Historic Glacier National Park*.

CPSIA information can be obtained
at www.ICGtesting.com
Printed in the USA
BVHW060030040321
601647BV00001B/1